LANDMARK COLLECTOR'S LIBRARY

The Spirit of
PENLEY:1
The 20th Century in Photographs

Derrick & Shirley Pratt

DIMICO PRO REGE

Bibliography

Files of the *Whitchurch Herald* and *Border Counties Advertiser*

HANMER, Sir John, Bart.
Memorial of the Parish of Hanmer (1871)

PRATT, D.
Church of St Mary Magdalene, Penley (1980)

PRATT, D.
Maelor in Times Past (1972)

PRATT, D.
A Pictorial History of Ellesmere and District 1790-1950 (1983)

PRATT, D.
"Penley as an Independent Parish" *Shropshire Family History Journal, XVI/4,* 133-137 (1995)

PRATT, D.
"Penley's Struggle for Independence Continues" *Shropshire Family History Journal, XVII/1,* 18-22 (1996)

PRATT, D. AND S.E.
A Vanished Heraldic Window (1990)

PRATT, S.E
The Dymocks of Penley or Llannerch Banna: A Family Pedigree (1989)

PRATT, S.E. and D.
A Millennium History of Penley (2000)

Acknowledgements

The compilation of these two pictorial books on Penley is based on some fifteen years of collecting, borrowing and copying images from a large number of people, both long time residents of the parish and relatively new 'incomers', as well as from family members who have moved away. For those pictures in Part 1, as far as memory permits the authors' thanks are due to the following: the late John Adams, Mrs Doreen Arthur, Mrs Audrey Brown, Clwyd Powys Archaeological Trust, Robert Cooper, the late Gilbert Evans, Mrs Margaret Evans, Stan and Joyce Evison, Flintshire Record Office, the late Arthur Fowles, Mrs Gladys Fowles, the late Jerzy Glen, Mrs Sallie Groom, Stanley Horton, Mrs Mary Huxley, Jon James, Mrs Sylvia Kinsey, late Mrs Violet Kulas, late Mrs Elsie Lloyd, late Sydney Lunt, James Machin, former Manpower Services (Clwyd County Council), Neville Metcalfe, Mrs Hilary Morris, National Assembly of Wales, Miss Margaret Owen, Mrs Mary Roberts, late Arch Rodenhurst, Glyn Rodenhurst, Doug Rolfe, late Mrs Mabel Rolfe, Mrs Joyce Sadowski, Mr and Mrs Rodney Spurr, Mrs Jean Summers, Miss Connie Tomlinson Mrs Joan Vernon, Mrs Haf Zamojska.

If any name has been inadvertently omitted, our apologies. You know who you are, and our sincerest thanks are due to you, no less than those named above.

LANDMARK COLLECTOR'S LIBRARY

THE SPIRIT OF
PENLEY:1

THE 20TH CENTURY IN PHOTOGRAPHS

Derrick & Shirley Pratt

Landmark Publishing

Published by

Ashbourne Hall, Cokayne Ave
Ashbourne, Derbyshire DE6 1EJ England
Tel: (01335) 347349 Fax: (01335) 347303
e-mail: landmark@clara.net
web site: www.landmarkpublishing.co.uk

1st edition

ISBN 1 84306 088 4

Printed by Bath Press Ltd, Bath

Design & reproduction by James Allsopp

Cover captions:

Front cover: Building Penley Parish Church, November, 1900
Back cover Top: May pole dancing, Penley, 1912
Back cover Middle: Corn harvest at Dymock Arms, 1921
Back cover Bottom: Shooting party, 1930

Page 1: Dymock coat-of-arms

Page 3: Inspection by the King and Queen of the 2nd Warszawska
Armoured Division colours embarkation in Scotland, 1945.

CONTENTS

INTRODUCTION

Today Penley is a pleasant, rapidly expanding dormitory village at the SE extremity of Wrexham County Borough. Its beginnings are lost in the mists of time, although the place-name hearkens back to the veneration accorded Penda, king of the Mercians (AD632-654). This book is a tale of two villages, the one an historic rural backwater, peripheral to the Domesday manor and mother church of Ellesmere in north Shropshire, and the other a settlement which had greatness, fame, even notoriety, thrust upon it in World War 2, and its aftermath. Whilst making for some social dislocation and readjustment, wartime happenings are not only the stuff from which legend is made, but are directly responsible for the opening up of the village to outside influences and to new blood, and indirectly have provided the spring-board from which Penley confidently advances into the 21st century.

One hundred years ago the casual traveller through the Welsh border country would have discerned in Penley a settlement little different from hundreds of other rural communities, spiritually drained and financially exhausted after a 30-year campaign to build a new parish church, seemingly impervious to further change, with not even the strength or will to repudiate the questing flutterings of Nonconformist sects and quietly stagnating about its new church, famous primary school and two pubs. Only occasionally, as the whim moved an individual farmer, did the community take on board advances in agricultural science and mechanisation.

Perhaps it was given impetus by the arrival of the railway, albeit technically 100 yards outside the parish boundary, which linked Penley with the greater world outside. New blood came and went, to the Vicarage, School House, and the 'big house', the latter's tenants automatically shouldering the social obligations of an historic squirearchy whose male line, like so many others, was suddenly snuffed out on the Flanders battlefields.

Penley struggled and seemingly was more poverty-stricken than most. There was no compact nucleated village, but rather what geographers would call a polyfocal settlement, each minor node responding to one of the string of commons, or wastes - Lightwood Green, Chapel Green, Far or Big Green - threaded out along the present A539, an ancient drovers' road, but today the principal caravan route between the Potteries and North Wales. The commons were enclosed by an Act of Parliament in 1796, leaving behind a distinctive 'squatter' settlement pattern.

In 1974, the Welsh Office mantra 'bigger is better' ushered in the first round in Local Government re-organisation in which the Tudor counties of Flintshire and Denbighshire were merged to form the new rather unwieldy entity of Clwyd. Ten years later, at grass roots level, the civil parish of Penley was grouped with Bettisfield to form the community of Maelor South thus retaining a sentimental onomastic link with the ancient district or Hundred of Maelor Saesneg ('English Maelor'), the largest of the several detached portions that made up the county of Flint. Despite incompatability, the Hundred of Maelor was forced into a shotgun union with councils west of the River Dee to give a hybrid tertiary authority known clumsily as Wrexham-Maelor. A further bout of reorganisation in 1996 saw Maelor South an integral part of a newly constituted Wrexham County Borough that has twice been denied 'city' status. In that Maelor shares long boundaries with Cheshire and Shropshire, the region's orientation has historically been eastwards into England rather than inland into Wales 'proper'. This applies particularly to Penley.

Such changes have left the village untouched physically. In 1984, in a rare piece of rationalisation, the projecting 'panhandle' of the adjacent township of Halghton was included within Penley 'ward' in Maelor South, thus acknowledging officially something which the local populace had long recognised - the concept of an 'extended village' of Penley. The western side of Cumbers ('short, shallow, broad, valley') Brook at Stryt Lydan, will indeed, mark the start of our pictorial odyssey through and about Penley.

Changes imposed unilaterally from above were something to which the village had resigned itself for over half a century. The earliest shifting of boundaries came in 1920 with the Disestablishment of the Church in Wales, the biggest appropriation of assets by government since the Dissolution of the Monasteries, a politically expedient hatchet job, as a result of which the ecclesiastical parish of Penley, for the best part of a millennium the only Welsh parish in the rural deanery of Ellesmere and archdeaconry of Shrewsbury in the diocese of Lichfield, was transferred kicking and screaming to the diocese of St. Asaph and the rural deanery of Bangor Isycoed in the archdeaconry of Wrexham. This involved a token change in spiritual allegiance.

Penley may be said to have toppled into the 20th century in 1942, when two sprawling United States Army hospitals were built in the parkland of the local big houses, Penley Hall (No.129 General Hospital with 1,000 beds) and Llannerch Panna (No.83 Station Hospital with 800 beds). It was not just a matter of the natives being suddenly outnumbered four-fold by an influx of American soldiers, with all attendant social problems and adjustments. On the plus side Penley's substandard roads and lanes, badly cut up by contractors' traffic, were almost overnight repaired and upgraded to almost urban standards. Electricity would however not reach those parts of the village the hospitals did not reach until 1952.

Once gained, such largesse in the way of an enhanced infrastructure and vastly diversified occupational base was not to be lightly discarded. Following the departure of the Americans in July 1945 Penley's two hospitals or 'camps' were occupied by a quick succession of British Army holding units. Then in August 1946 'the Poles' arrived in the shape of detachments of the Polish Resettlement Corps, with former Polish Army field hospitals in tow - No.11 Polish Hospital to Llannerch Panna, No.3 Polish Hospital to Penley Hall, the latter duly absorbing No.4 Polish (TB) Hospital from Iscoyd, upon retrenchment in 1956.

Thus began Penley's indelible association with Polish exiles, as 'a little Polonia beyond Wales'. As these 'camps' have in turn closed - No.11 in 1953 and No.3, duty to all but eight monoglot Polish patients finally done, in 2002 - Penley has inherited useful pieces of real estate allocated for housing, a small industrial park, and a new 'state of the art' community hospital, work on which commenced in May 2003. Earlier plans for warehousing, even an open prison, on No.11, came to nothing, while proposals to utilise the 'brown field' site for a brand new bilateral or comprehensive school to serve Maelor, were modified in favour of building on an ill-drained 'green field' site along the main road. On the Maelor School has fallen the mantle of boosting Penley's profile in the wider world beyond the Dee, aided and abetted by the village's cottage ornée Madras School, the first National School in Wales (1811) and, strong winds permitting, still carrying a thatched roof!

Stryt Lydan, harvest group, 1920. *L-r:*
Charlie Want (gamekeeper), Henry Rolfe, ?, John Jefferies, Edward Evans, Albert Evans.

STRYT LYDAN

1

Having crossed the deep broad valley of Cumbers Brook from the Hanmer direction, the first buildings one comes across on the Penley side are those associated with the outlying hamlet of Stryt Lydan ('broad street'), possibly so called because of a suspected Roman origin, or, which is the more likely, because the highway did indeed widen after being restricted by the pale of the medieval deer park in Park Lane.

Stryt Lydan Smithy c.1910. Situated at a convenient cross roads, equidistant between smithies at Hanmer, Bradenheath, Sandy Lane and Halghton and serving a dozen or so farms and smallholdings, the outlying portion of the Dymock (Penley Hall) estate. It became a smithy in 1843 when Stephen Evans (blacksmith) moved here from Bronington. It remained in the hands of the Evans family until 5 May 1903 when there was a contents sale. Later in 1903 Phil Edge moved here from Sandy Lane smithy, Penley. He is seen standing in the doorway with his son Bernard (in shirtsleeves). His wife Martha ran a small grocery shop from the cottage, hence the visit of Grooms's trap, the latter bakers and confectioners of Bronington.

In such a smithy one existed almost at subsistence level. Stephen Evans ran five dairy cows. Latterly smithying declined as horse numbers dwindled. The Summers family eked out an uneasy existence as smallholders before giving up under pressure from large scale operators and a burgeoning bureaucracy.

Above left: Martha Edge, who ran a grocery shop attached to both Sandy Lane and Stryt Lydan smithies. *Above right:* Smithying probably finished at Stryt Lydan sometime before the death of Phil Edge in 1937 at the age of 83. Thereafter, small-scale farming. Three churns of milk daily to United Dairies, Ellesmere. Phil Summers with elder son Neil, c.1952. Today, Neil is a successful antiques dealer!

Above left: Even smallholdings had to mechanise. Phil Summers and Simon (grandson) in 1972 with David Brown tractor, of 1947-53 vintage. *Above right:* Stryt Lydan Smithy as a private house before the Summers family moved out in 1987. Former smith's shop to right. *Right:* No room on the small farm for a younger son. Nigel Summers moved into local government.. Here on 3 December 2002, as CEO of Sandwell, West Midlands, he receives his CBE at Buckingham Palace for services to 'regeneration'.

Above: Stryt Lydan, a splendid farmhouse on the north side of the road as Park Lane is approached. It has stood alone since 'Dairy House Farm' across the road was demolished c.1868. Stryt Lydan is a late Georgian building, a single unit when lived in by gentleman farmers with large families, but frequently subdivided to provide accommodation for farm manager or bailiff. Here the house is seen in 1919, dressed overall with flags and laurel arch on the occasion of a family wedding. The farm of some 136 acres formerly belonged to the Dymock estate, but in 1891 was purchased by Frederick Jefferies. It became part of the Gredington estate in 1948.

Below: The Jefferies daughters married into other Penley or Halghton farming 'dynasties', Chapel House, The Pant, but they had to get their hands dirty. Here in 1923 are the considerable work forces needed to run the Stryt Lydan dairy and 'milking parlour'. Back row l-r: Sarah Mary Jefferies, Fred Green, John Jefferies, Percy Simpson, Jack Thompson; front row, l-r: Elsie Jefferies, Dolly Simpson, Frances Jefferies, Vera Jefferies, Cissie Thompson. Note the clogs being worn by the girls.

The Stryt Lydan daughters are obviously of a well-to-do farming family, even at a period when agriculture was depressed.

Above left: Mary Jane, daughter of Frederick and Sarah Jefferies, 1896.
Above right: Margaret Jefferies, 1913.
Below left: Frances and Elsie Jefferies, 1922.
Below right: Hazel, daughter of John and Vera Jefferies, 1930.

Above: Ready for social calls, 1913. Maggie Jefferies (standing), Frances, Sarah Mary (mother) and Elsie Jefferies, with 'Dolly', the horse.

Below: 1920. Horse and trap have given way to a brand new motor car. From left: Jack Thompson, Percy Simpson, Sarah Jefferies, Cissie Thompson and Dolly Simpson (compare with earlier picture of the dairy workers!).

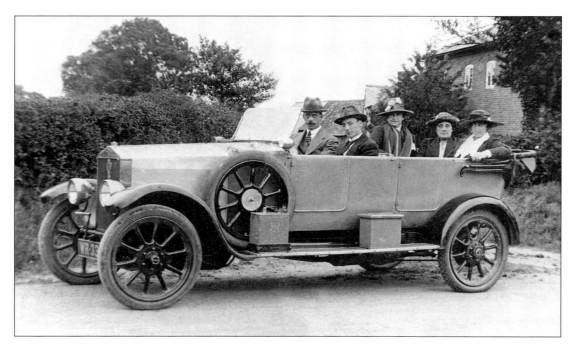

Above: 1920. Stryt Lydan wedding group: Margaret Jefferies and John Kynaston, who would take over the Pant. Back row, l-r: Mary Jefferies, John Kynaston (groom's father), Jennie Kynaston (groom's stepmother), John Kynaston (groom), Sarah Mary Jefferies (bride's mother), Margaret Jefferies (bride) Evelyn Jefferies, Dolly Simpson, Ellen Rolfe; seated, l-r: John Jefferies, Frances Jefferies, William Griffiths (best man), Mary Jane Jefferies; front, l-r: Elsie Jefferies (see next photograph), Leslie Green. John Kynaston, senior, was butler to Lord Kenyon and lived at the Pigeon House.

Below: Elsie Jefferies turn (she was bridesmaid in above photograph). She wed Harold Lloyd whose father then kept the 'Hanmer Arms', Hanmer. They would later take over Adra-felin farm. Back row, l-r: Cissie Thompson, Frank Griffiths, Mrs. Winsbury, Rev. Canon Chambers (Hanmer), Frances Griffiths, John Leadsom, Sarah Mary Jefferies, Joe Craige, Catherine Craige, Leigh Lloyd, Madge Craige; front row, l-r: Eileen Williams, Mary Williams, Fred Jefferies, Leslie Lloyd, Evelyn Lloyd (bridesmaid) Harold Lloyd (groom), Elsie Jefferies (bride), Frank Lloyd (best man), Hazel Jefferies, Evelyn Leadsom, Mrs. Chambers; forefront: Iris Jefferies, Myra Williams (bridesmaid).

That Stryt Lydan was several notches up the farming scale is indicated by the enormous barn that once stood at the back of the house. Of cruck and box frame construction, this barn was capable of storing an entire crop of wheat, oats and barley without ricking in the open fields. But after 1870, with the shift from arable to dairying it became redundant and condemned to inevitable decay, perhaps even demolition. By 1948 cows were being milked on the ground floor while the whole had been lofted for hay. In 1949 Lord Kenyon offered the building as the first outdoor exhibit in the newly established Welsh Folk Museum, St. Fagans. It was duly dismantled and re-erected in Cardiff over 1950-51.

Above: The oldest (c.1550) section of the Penley Barn, alias that at Stryt Lydan, seen in 1949 prior to dismantling. Wattle-and-daub panels had given way (c.1750) to brick nogging and/or weather boarding and planking. The thatched roof has disappeared, but timely reslating by the Gredington estate has prevented further dilapidation.

Opposite page; Top: The 'Penley Barn', February 1950. Dismantling in progress. Original three-bay cruck barn, open drift house and later (c.1650) box frame addition are clearly shown. The brick gable end is later, as are the sill foundations and were not salvaged, but rebuilt in limestone.
Bottom: The raising of the Stryt Lydan barn's No.4 cruck at St. Fagan's, 1950. The new limestone plinth is already in place.

Detail of cruck No.4 (drift house original north wall), fully framed, with cruck blades set on sill beams resting on low sleeper stone wall. Blades meet on a king post rising from a collar and are held together by a yoke. Being a gable cruck it has framing members below the tie beam.

16

A carefully restored box frame (drift house original south wall) on the later part of the barn. This section of the barn came from somewhere else and may never have been wattled after being added, although wattled infill panels have been added upon reconstruction. Note that panel staves run horizontally and cleft pieces vertically. The doors are seemingly too small for stock other than calves.

Above: The Stryt Lydan barn at St. Fagan's in 1994, the 3-bay cruck section (14m long, 5.4m wide, 5.8m high) to the right. The missing end (No.1) cruck has been replaced by a limestone wall.
Below: Looking at the barn from the smaller box-framed section, the irregular plinth would seem to indicate that the timbers were re-used from at least one, probably two, other buildings.

PARK LANE

3

Between Stryt Lydan and the cross-roads in Penley stretches Park Lane, so called because in Tudor times it ran along the southern edge of a medieval deer park, still recalled by the survival of Big Park, Little Park and several Parks as field names. In 1458 the park emerges from the records as Park y gwernor (Parke y gwino 1634), a reference either to 'park of the large alder-moor' or to the park's 'palisade of alder'. There was no settlement on the former parkland. Farmhouses, stackyards, orchards, barns and outbuildings are lined up together on the south side of the road almost like the German Strassendorf or 'street village'. There would have been a seventh farm to add to this unique settlement complex, but 'Dairy House Farm' was demolished c.1868. The half-timbered, box-framed, brick-nogged Park Lane barns, still retaining traces of the original undaubed wattle panels have been dated to the early 16th century. The farmhouses, although externally reclad, may have been of this date too. No.4 Park Lane was demolished in 1951-2 without being properly recorded.

Left: Park Lane, looking east, 1910. No.2 is in the foreground. The road is hardly recognisable as the present A539. Subsequent widening has taken away ditch and hedge on the left hand side, possibly relict traces of the park's boundary pale. No.2 has clearly had its roof lines raised to accommodate dormers. In 1851 one Asher Ashley, head of a large family of slaters and plasterers, lived at No.2 Park Lane and later at No.5 and Dairy House Farm and Halghton Grove. Asher was a proselytizing Methodist and set up cottage prayer meetings at each and every one of his homes.

Right: A second view of Park Lane, 1910, looking beyond No.4 to No.5. The farmhouse is fronted by an original barn, very much dilapidated. Note the ground-floor 'cellar' at the side of the house carries a huge thatched roof!

Above: No.5 Park Lane, 1920, with Evelyn Leadsom standing in the doorway. Until 1957 No.5 was part of the Gredington estate.

Left: John and Evelyn Leadsom (née Jefferies), tenants of No.5 in 1925.

Below: Relatives call in style. William and Mary Elizabeth Leadsom (from No.3 Park Lane) in pony and trap in the yard of No.5, 1929.

No.5 Park Lane in 1937. Albert Evans and son John, in advertising pose outside farm buildings, endorsing Levers cattle meal and an Alfa Laval milking machine.

Opposite page: For most of the 20th century, following the final break up of the Dymock estate, No.4 Park Lane has been in the hands of the Williams family. Fred and Mary Jane Williams (née Jefferies) in 1921.

Above: Christmas Day, 1946. Edna Williams outside pantry/scullery of the old house. The interior walls of No.4 contained wattle-and-daub panels.

Right: Mary Jane Williams at the gate of No.4 in 1948. Shortly afterwards the house was demolished.

The 16th century barn at No.4 Park Lane, as seen from the road, was built in two main parts, the box framed 2-bay section, one bay larger than the other, with lower panels filled in with brick and loft panels covered by weather boarding, in October 1980 very much the worse for wear.

The same barn, viewed from the stackyard. A later 3-bay brick section has been added, uniformity given by an overall thatched roof, replaced, first by a slate roof, and then
by the ubiquitous corrugated iron sheeting, retaining ridge tiles from the slate roof.

Close-up of the west gable, minus farming clutter. The end frame has full height timbers. Some time in the 19th century an attempt has been made to replace the timber sill.

Above: No.3 Park Lane, 1910. Hannah Roberts, widow of Joseph Roberts (1906), standing behind the hedge. Note position of front door.
Left: Family group at No.3 Park Lane, 1932. Seated: Mary Elizabeth and William Leadsom; standing: Arthur John Fowles and Louisa Hobbs, with 'Shep' the dog.
Below: No.3 Park Lane, 1992. Note the house had been altered - front door has been moved into the middle of the elevation and an enclosed porch erected. New windows have been provided over all.

Above: Compared with the picture on p.19 No.2 Park Lane has been modernised since it changed hands in 1987. It is now given over to the raising of rarer breeds of cattle.

Above: 'Hawthorn Villa', otherwise No.1 Park Lane, was built c.1950 replacing the original cottage of which no complete picture exists. Disintegrating exterior brickwork eventually proved impossible to repair.

Left: Frances and Dorothy, daughters of John Thomas and Winifred Hannah Lunt, stand outside the back door of No.1 Park Lane in 1905, obviously, judging from brickwork, the cottage needed quite a lot doing to it.

Above: The last building to be associated with the medieval park was today's 'Dymock Arms' pub. In this 'exploded' view, if one removes the east (right-hand) end of 1920, and the west (left-hand) end of c.1870 we are left with two keepers' cottages in the centre. They had become an ale house or pub known as 'The Plough' by 1600, but the partition wall still contains original timbers and wattle-and-daub panels.

Below: Following the laying of the first in 1884, a second Lake Vyrnwy-Liverpool pipeline was put down in 1905. Here the work gang crosses the 'Dymock's meadow (otherwise the Hempbutt) at the west end of the former park in September 1904. Here were located the meters for the various private water mains that took Liverpool water to the conveniently placed 'big houses' up to five miles distant. Some navvies were billeted locally but most slept rough in the pipes. When the next pipeline came through in the late 1940s the contractors were better organised with the workforce housed in mobile hutted camps.

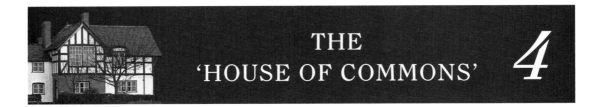

THE 'HOUSE OF COMMONS'

4

The essential spirit of a place over history is encapsulated in its church, chapel, pub, and school, not necessarily in that order. Penley is no exception and each will be considered in turn as far as pictorial sources permit. Of Penley's three former ale-houses, 'The Dymock Arms', formerly 'The Plough', has fared better than the opposition. Currently (December 2002) it is undergoing yet another structural face-lift, so what better reason than for a little nostalgia?

The Dymock Arms, 1915. The pub is possibly the second oldest building in Penley. Richard Latham (landlord 1902-1925), his second wife Hilda and family are standing alongside the hedge. The single storey extension was known as the 'Long Room', where rent dinners etc. were held.

Above: The Dymock Arms, 1922, with new (1920) extension on the right. The giant horse chestnut towering over the roof line is in full leaf. Regretfully it would be felled in 1927.

Above: The Dymock Arms, 1922, close-up of the new extension with single story bottle store to the rear. As seen in the next picture, the Long Room was not completely demolished but incorporated in the shell of the new extension.

Right: The 'Top Room' during alterations June 1999. Plasterboard has been stripped off the walls to reveal that original vertical timbers of the Long Room had been preserved, possibly as strengthening timbers.

Trade card (1928) produced by Charles Evans who had taken over as landlord in 1925, following the retirement of Richard Latham.

THE DYMOCK ARMS,
PENLEY, Near ELLESMERE, Salop.

Fully Licensed.   *Luncheons and Teas Provided.*

CHARLES EVANS, Proprietor.

The Dymock Estate rent dinner 1933, held twice a year, May and November. Once a year the squire, Rowland Griffith Vaughton Dymock attended. Lady tenants attended the rent dinners but were not permitted to dine with the men. They ate in the kitchen! Back row, l-r: Fred Owen (Old Post Office), Harold Reece (Lower House), Bill Leadsome (Vicarage Lane), Ern Tomlinson (The Grange), Tom Leadsom (Little Green), Ern Williams (Bridge House), Harry Breslin (Croxton Pool), Henry (chauffeur); front row, l-r: Phil Edge (Stryt Lydan Smithy), Charles Evans (Dymock Arms), Mr. Warburton-Lee of Broad Oak (agent), Rowland Griffith Vaughton Dymock (squire) ,...?..., Sidney Preston (Halghton Grove).

Thursday, June 22nd, 1939,

AT 11-30 A.M.

DYMOCK ARMS HOTEL & FARM
PENLEY,

9 miles from Whitchurch, 4 miles from Ellesmere, 3 miles from
Overton-on-Dee on the Hanmer main road.

Important Unreserved Dispersal Sale of

54 Friesian and Shorthorn Cross Dairy Cattle

YOUNG STOCK & BULLS.

Two Grand Work Horses.

50 Utility Poultry.

A First-Class Selection of Modern Farm Implements

LURRIES. CARTS. GEARS.

DAIRY UTENSILS. CHEESE MAKING APPARATUS.

Poultry Houses & Appliances.

Household Furniture and Effects.

Henry Manley & Sons, Ltd.

(*R. Manley, F.A.I., & E. E. Wright, F.A.I.*)

Are favoured with instructions from Mr. Charles Evans (who is giving up
the tenancy owing to ill-health) to conduct this unreserved sale.

Luncheons and Licensed Refreshments.

Catalogues from the Auctioneers' Offices: Whitchurch (Tel. 19 & 357),
Crewe (Tel 2654 & 2651), and Branches.

The Dymock Arms was also a working farm,, with 55 acres attached. The dispersal sale catalogue,
1939, upon retirement of Charles Evans as landlord.

Above: Corn harvest on the Dymock's farm, 1921. Dick Latham, then tenant, on binder holding Ethel, ...?..., Edward Evans ('Little Ted'), Horace Latham with dog, John Latham on horse.

Below: The Dymock Arms, 1952. Taken by a Manchester photographic agency intent on compiling a portfolio of UK pubs that spanned the 'two Elizabeths'! They had documentary evidence to prove the Dymock's pedigree!, and, as will be seen below, confined their photography to the oldest parts of the pub.

The Dymock Arms, 1952. 'Kitchen' bar, original timbers, although the inglenook has been modernised with a boiler/oven range installed by Birchall & Son, Whitchurch in 1888. The left-hand hob carries a copper 'Dolphin' beer filter.

Serving hatch in the 'Kitchen' bar. In a man's world, the long ash settle and two oak screen settles were not made for comfort. The highly polished oak tables were ideal for scuffling dominoes. In later years, the stripping of nearly ten layers of wallpaper would expose the original timber beams.

The Dymock Arms, the farmhouse kitchen or living room, plain, functional. The ceiling has been raised at an unknown date.

The Dymock Arms, 1963, showing its dual function as a pub and working farm. Farm buildings and stackyard to left, pig sty, tractor shed and orchard to rear. The cottage beyond, now 'Dymock Cottage', was once 'The Old Post Office'. The ground floor front of the six-bay shippon is faced in brick but to the rear and inside the Elizabethan timbers of the box frame were exposed as good as new, only to be dismantled and burnt c.1980 to make room for a car park extension.

Pub work, farm work, domestic chores - all the same to George Evans, seen here dressing and cleaning guinea fowl, 1963.

A sight no longer seen on UK farms. On the Dymock Arms front, 1958. Loading the United Dairies (Ellesmere) wagon with standard 10-gallon milk churns, each weighing over 110 lbs, is George Peate.

A break from 'mucking out' - Cyril Crewe (used to cycle from Manchester for a holiday!), and Gilbert and George Evans rest on their forks, 1938.

Against a back drop of beer barrels and milk churns, Florence Evans, matriarch of farm and pub, 1938, the year before she retired to Minsterley, Shropshire.

THE SUNDAY OPENING QUESTION

CHAPTER 61.

An Act to prohibit the Sale of Intoxicating Liquors on Sunday in Wales. [27th August 1881.]

A.D. 1881.

WHEREAS the provisions in force against the sale of fermented and distilled liquors during certain hours of Sunday have been found to be attended with great public benefits, and it is expedient and the people of Wales are desirous that in the principality of Wales those provisions be extended to the other hours of Sunday :

Be it therefore enacted by the Queen's most Excellent Majesty, by and with the advice and consent of the Lords Spiritual and Temporal, and Commons, in this present Parliament assembled, and by the authority of the same, as follows :

1. In the principality of Wales all premises in which intoxicating liquors are sold or exposed for sale by retail shall be closed during the whole of Sunday.

Premises where intoxicating liquors sold to be closed on Sundays in Wales.

2. The Licensing Acts, 1872–1874, shall apply in the case of any premises closed under this Act as if they had been closed under those Acts.

Application of Licensing Acts.
35 & 36 Vict. c. 94.
37 & 38 Vict. c. 49.

3. This Act shall commence and come into operation with respect to each division or place in Wales on the day next appointed for the holding of the general annual licensing meeting for that division or place.

Commencement of Act.

4. Nothing in this Act contained shall preclude the sale at any time at a railway station of intoxicating liquors to persons arriving at or departing from such station by railway.

Sale of intoxicating liquors at railway stations.

5. This Act may be cited as the Sunday Closing (Wales) Act, 1881.

Short title.

LONDON: Printed by George Edward Eyre and William Spottiswoode Printers to the Queen's most Excellent Majesty. 1881.

[*Public.—61.*]

In the 1960s the question of Sunday opening of licensed premises in Wales engaged the minds of serious drinkers everywhere. It took three referendums to settle the problem. In the first round of 8 November 1961 only Flintshire in North Wales voted 'Wet' (with a majority of 10,176). Accordingly on 12 November 1961 the Dymock Arms opened on Sunday for the first time since 1881. Further polls on 6 Novemebr 1968 and 5 November 1975 saw the rest of the country embrace Sunday opening.

The sign above the porch of the Dymock tells its own story. 'Closed on Sunday' has been masked off. The sign has just been repainted (not as a celebration) by J. Bramwell & Son, Gobowen, at a cost of £30.

In 1966 the outside world caught up with Penley as, using his ancestral connections, finally severed in 1950, John Dymock Maunsell, brought the Rolls Royce Club of Great Britain to the Dymock Arms for a pit stop on their way to the Rolls Royce works at Crewe.

Left: The 1936 Bentley owned by John Dymock Maunsell, which was used by his grandfather when he attended rent dinners at Penley. It carries a silver 'Dymock's' lion above the windscreen.

Middle: Busy industrialist Sir Basil Ferranti had his chauffeur drive his Rolls to Penley whilst he himself flew in by helicopter to complete the final leg to Crewe.

Below left: Basil Ferranti behind the wheel of his 'Silver Ghost', then worth three times more than his helicopter! *Below right:* What is the collective noun for an assemblage of Rolls Royce cars? A 'pride' of RR's outside the Dymocks.

In 1967 John Dymock Maunsell repeated the PR exercise, this time bringing members of the Vintage Rolls Royce Club of America onto the pub forecourt for drinks. All cars have left-hand drive.

Shropshire - Flintshire Borders

THE RENOWNED DAIRY AND STOCK FARMS

known as

THE DYMOCK ARMS and PENLEY HALL FARMS

Penley, Near Ellesmere

Extending to approximately

224 ACRES

AND OFFERED IN SIX LOTS

With Vacant Possession

PUGH & PURSELL

have been instructed to offer the above for sale by Public Auction

AT THE PARISH HALL, PENLEY

On THURSDAY, 20th OCTOBER, 1966, at 7 p.m.

(subject to conditions)

Auctioneers :	Solicitor :
PUGH & PURSELL,	E. A. WHITEHEAD, Esq.,
The Square, Ellesmere (Tel. 402), and at	127/131, The Albany,
Moorlands House, 3/4, Shoplatch, Shrewsbury	Old Hall Street,
(Tel. 4482/3).	Liverpool, 3 (Tel. CEN 8289).

Following the death of George Evans in July 1966, the pub and farms were taken over by his widow and daughter.

Left: Sales catalogue. The smaller Dymock Arms Farm was sold on 20 October 1966. Penley Hall farm was let.

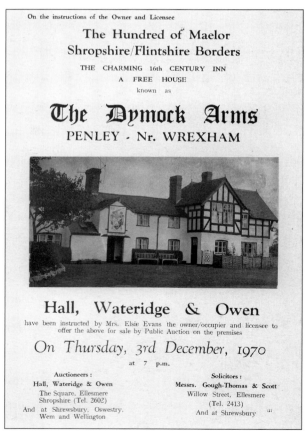

On the instructions of the Owner and Licensee

The Hundred of Maelor
Shropshire/Flintshire Borders

THE CHARMING 16th CENTURY INN

A FREE HOUSE

known as

The Dymock Arms
PENLEY - Nr. WREXHAM

Hall, Wateridge & Owen

have been instructed by Mrs. Elsie Evans the owner/occupier and licensee to offer the above for sale by Public Auction on the premises

On Thursday, 3rd December, 1970

at 7 p.m.

Auctioneers :	Solicitors :
Hall, Wateridge & Owen	Messrs. Gough-Thomas & Scott
The Square, Ellesmere	Willow Street, Ellesmere
Shropshire (Tel. 2602)	(Tel. 2413)
And at Shrewsbury, Oswestry,	And at Shrewsbury
Wem and Wellington	

The pub itself was finally sold on 3 December 1970, the new landlords taking over on 5 April 1971.

Meanwhile a woman's touch had made a difference to the 'kitchen' bar seen here in 1970 replete with brasses and the original Penley Hall phosphor-bronze bell of 1807, which used to call Penley folk to and from work at 6am and 6pm.

The grate in the farmhouse kitchen had also undergone a face-lift. The range was supplied and installed by W.H. Smith & Sons, Whitchurch and apparently was originally 'silver plated' overall, not just knobs and strap hinges. Must have been a wonderful sight. What went wrong that it is now seen black-leaded, a daily chore?

'The Dymocks' filled a changing community role as the week progressed:

Early Thursday evening, before the farmers came in, was traditionally a time when the world was set to rights. Here the local 'schoolboss ' holds centre stage. Left to right: Frank Lloyd, Frank Cotton & Derrick Pratt.

In an age before wall to wall muszak or juke boxes, the kitchen bar made its own music. Harvey Evans was better on the house accordion than the guitar!, 'Johnnie' Walsh (left).

Left: For seven years after Flintshire 'went wet' in 1961 the top room at the Dymocks became the weekend haunt of sections of the Rhos Male Voice Choir.

Below: In the 1960s local elections, if contested, were hard fought campaigns, that inevitably concluded at the Dymock Arms. Here, in 1966, the successful candidate has a 'cow chain' of office thrust upon him by grinning supporters. Left to right: Bill Groom, Derrick Pratt & Idris Roberts.

1958. George Evans, Elsie May Evans and daughter Shirley Elizabeth Evans who ran the 'Dymocks', July 1939-April 1971.

Above: Seen before the reconstruction of 2002 got underway. The 'Pool Room' with timbers from the original 'Long Room' tastefully retained.

Opposite page; Top: A new lounge bar in the dining area occupies what was a wine and spirits store, and before that a cheese-making room.
Bottom: The 'middle bar', beams and walls have been sand-blasted. The low beams mark the extent of the 16th century cottage which had its end wall knocked out in 1920.

AT THE CROSS ROADS 5

The crossroads, with its pub, shop, post office, filling station and various small housing schemes, is the hub of the village today. But before enclosure in 1796 the whole of the area shown was common land - Big Green or Far Green. The lanes are all medieval: to Halghton (top right); noting bend to take the track around the pub and farm, originally the park keepers' cottage(s). The Back Lane, (running off bottom centre), gave access to the rear fields of the various Park Lane farms, but by 1387 had been continued to Hampton's Wood and Welshhampton in Shropshire. Ellesmere Lane (bottom left corner) owes its initial straightness to the enclosure commissioner's ruler, but then curves and twists via sunken hollow-ways, to the nearest market town - Ellesmere in Shropshire. Beneath the aeroplane's wing new housing marks the first steps in the redevelopment of the Penley Hall hospital site.

Today Penley is no different from any other rural community. Farmhouses continue to be alienated as non-agricultural private residences and the land attached to surrounding holdings. The Back Lane is a case in point having lost three farming units. Glebe Farm Cottage disappeared in 1875, The Grange went out of farming in 1986 and Lower Grange in 1980.

Left: The Grange, 1963, Florence Mary Tomlinson standing in her front garden. The house is early 19th century with splendid mutular Doric porch and original 6-panel door with radial bar fanlight. The house was probably built by the Briscoes, one of Penley's most respected yeoman farming families, whose vault still exists in the closed part of the churchyard.

Right: The Grange, 1998, refurbished and no longer part of the agricultural scene.

Left: The Grange, 1998. The living room retains original exposed beams to ceiling, but the feature fireplace has been enhanced by timbers from elsewhere.

53

Lower Grange in the Back Lane, is typical of the many Penley smallholdings that have been 'retired' from farming and converted into private residences, with or without land attached.

Above: Lower Grange in 1972, granary and shippon to left.
Below: In 1837 there were only 20 acres attached to the Lower Grange. Thomas Sadler had to eke out his farming activities as a builder. Here, in 1921, the Lower Grange is an ideal first rung on the farming ladder. Sydney Preston had married in 1914 and would later move to a much larger place at Halghton Grove. Children Reginald and Mary up.

Above: Lower Grange, 1994, after conversion. Front door has been moved; garden hedge and wicket have disappeared, and windows inserted in all elevations of barn. Drift-way is new entrance. *Below:* In 1998 the farmhouse kitchen makes a comfortable living room, retaining original features or re-using old materials.

Cohesion is given to the crossroads by the former 'Ebenezer' Primitive Methodist Chapel, opened 28 September 1900 on a plot given by John Broomhall, Lower Grange. Prior to this, Dissenters had led a peripatetic existence in farms and cottages about the parish.

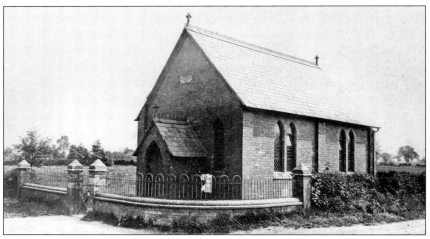

Top: 'Ebenezer' Chapel, 1920, Not a house in sight; built on the corner of Ellesmere Lane, by Price Williams, Penley, under a committee chaired by Jonathan Pierrepoint, Halghton Grove.

Middle: Rear view of 'Ebenezer' Chapel, looking down Ellesmere Lane towards Penley Hall parkland, later taken over by a US Army hospital. The lean-to building against the back wall of the chapel was, 1940-44, the HQ of Penley platoon, Home Guard.

Bottom: The chapel closed for worship in 1970, maintenance being beyond the limited resources of the few families left to support the cause in Penley. Seen here in 1988 when the chapel was being used as a leather-working craft centre.

The Old Chapel, 2002, tastefully converted into a private dwelling thus saving a little bit of Penley's architectural heritage.

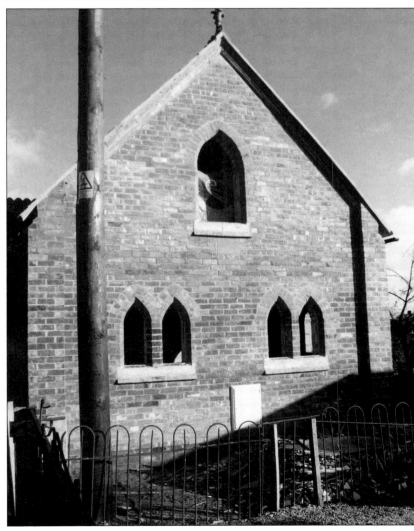

March, 2002. Building work is well under way with a small rear extension with 'chapel' style windows inserted.

A new floor has been inserted, reached by a reclaimed staircase.

A bedroom shows an original roof truss and the tips of the side elevation windows.

In addition to the present shop/Post Office, Penley has had four 'Old Post Offices' - rather confusing for researchers - one in Ellesmere Lane, one in Chapel House as was, and two at the south end of Halghton Lane, one of which has disappeared and the other modernised.

Top left: The Old Post Office, east side of Halghton lane, 1920. Formerly part of the Dymock estate, with 2 acres of land attached. Functioned as a Post Office 1903-1910. Gwen and Ethel (in pram) Latham in front of the cottage.

Top right: By 1912, the Old Post Office had become a tied cottage to Penley Hall farm, then in 1950 to the 'Dymock Arms' farm, and re-named 'Dymock's Cottage', seen here in 1972. New windows have been inserted, possibly scrounged from a redundant military building.

Left: 'Dymocks Cottage' from the rear, 1972, Older brickwork marks the size of the original 1837 cottage, when it was occupied by John Clay, wheelwright.

Right: By 1990 'Dymocks Cottage' has undergone a total transformation.

Left: Rear view of 'Dymock's Cottage after renovation, 1990.

Middle: The Old Post Office, north side of Halghton Lane in 1950 before demolition. A half-timbered cottage on the Dymock estate it became the Post Office between 1851-61. Cornelius and Emma Williams retired in 1901 after 24 years as Postmaster and Postmistress. The Post Office then moved temporarily to Chapel House.

Bottom left: The Old Post Office, 1947. This water-colour by S.W. Starling shows the cottage with a thatched roof.

Bottom right: The last occupant of the Old Post Office was Frederick Owen seen outside his cottage in 1955.

TO THE 'BIG HOUSE' 6

Ellesmere Lane ran onto the Big Green. In 1796 many of the cottages at the north end of the lane were marked as 'ancient enclosures', i.e. 'squatter' settlements, legitimate or otherwise. The lane was also the main approach to Penley House and its successor Llannerch Panna, the 'big house' after the eclipse of the Penley Hall dynasty and obviously afforded access to the American/Polish hospital.

Top left: First of the 'squatter' cottages - Yew Tree Cottage, 1910. Ernest Albert and Ellen Rolfe at the gate.
Top right: Yew Tree Cottage, 1914. Ernest Rolfe had a bicycle shop in the wooden hut, right. His son, Hugh, stands in front of the hedge. It was sold out of the Llannerch Panna estate in 1929.

Left: Ernest and Ellen Rolfe, Yew Tree Cottage, 1915. They moved to Whitchurch later that year. Sons Norman (left) and Hugh (right).

Old cottages with large gardens in a popular dormitory village were ripe for redevelopment.

Top left: 'Glanor', 1993, built on the of the original Yew Tree Cottage in the 1970s.

Top right: Auction details for 'Glanor', 1994, a vast cry from its predecessor.

Bottom left: 'Yew Trees', Ellesmere Lane, 1993, built in the garden of Yew Tree Cottage.

Bottom right: Auction details for 'Yew Trees', 1994.

Above: Standpipe Cottages, Ellesmere Lane, 1928. Two, later three, cottages, so called because its single tap or standpipe (between first door and second window) served all the cottages in the lane. The cottages were part of the Llannerch Panna estate 1876-1929. Henry Williams, from No.5 stands at the gap in the hedge and is obviously posing for the photographer whilst collecting water.

Right: In 1932 Margaret Speakman, 2 Standpipe Cottages, made headlines in Shropshire papers as passing her centenary. She was actually 102 when this photograph was taken. She was born in Ellesmere on 17 May 1830 and was buried at Penley 7 September 1933. Her husband, William, died in Penley in 1915, aged 85.

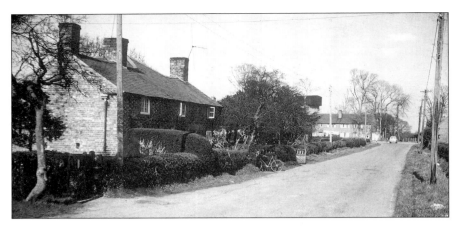

Above: Ellesmere Lane looking north, 1966. A typically straight enclosure road, whose broad grass verges have gradually been eroded by road widening. Standpipe Cottages to the left. The eponymous 'yew tree' masks the landmark water tower of Penley Hall hospital.

Right: Standpipe Cottages, 1988, shortly after conversion and modernisation. Three cottages have become a single residence.

Below: Even earlier the garden of No.2 Standpipe Cottages was lost to private building, notably 'Glenfern' and 'Lyndale', seen here in 1938. They were built by John Hale of Bishop's House.

Top left: No.5 Ellesmere Lane, 1988. A squatter's cottage in the second stage in a DIY modernisation programme. One gable chimney yet survives, but sagging ridge pieces still need attention.
Top right: Nos.4 & 5 Ellesmere Lane, 1969. Ann Osbourne (visitor) with 'Tiny' the cat. Two cottages clearly discernible. Doors and windows will be moved about or bricked up over the coming years.
Bottom left: Starting in 1972, Nos.4a & 5 Ellesmere Lane are now one. A door has been bricked up (marked by lines of garden path) as has also the ground floor window to right of door.
Bottom right: Four generations at No.5 in 1978. Annie Rodenhurst (seated) holding Gareth (great-grandson); Glyn (grandson) standing and 'Arch' Rodenhurst (son) seated right.

65

Above: The Post Office, Ellesmere Lane, 1943. In 1909 the then vicar of Penley (Rev. T.M. Burnett) sold a small piece of glebe land to William Owen, who had run a Post Office from Dymock's Cottage, Halghton Lane. The latter then built a house and Post Office on the land.

Below: The 'Old' Post Office, Ellesmere Lane, 1960, now a private residence. In 1955 postal business had been transferred to Chapel House again, whilst the present village stores, which would contain a Post Office counter, was being built.

Across the road from the Old Post Office stood the last of the 'ancient enclosures' which had sprung up on the extremities of 'Big Green'.

Left: Holly Cottage, Ellesmere Lane, 1980. In 1837 a single cottage, but in 1910 had been divided into two, with Myrtlewood having its entrance in the opposite elevation.

Right: Myrtlewood and Holly Cottages in 1988. They had been empty for some time.

Left: The same two cottages in 1992. They were sold separately. Myrtlewood was remodelled, but Holly Cottage was demolished and a new home built in its place.

Above: Big Green Farm, 1980. The name is a transferred one, the original farm also known as Fields Farm, being on the edge of common land but further NW behind Rangle Town. Farmhouse centre, 'Wilmaye' left, a modern bungalow replacing a 14th century cruck cottage, and a 1970s bungalow right.

Left: White Gates, 1945, a half-timbered cottage that once stood between the farmhouse and 'Wilmaye'. This cottage may have been the earliest encroachment on the Penley wastes.

Above: The gates and lodge to Llannerch Panna, 1930. In 1942 these gates would be swept away with the building of a US Army hospital in the grounds.

Above: The Lodge, 1960. Built in 1842 it was originally lodge to Penley House. A longer and more private drive to the estate, without a lodge, was provided off the main road when Llannerch Panna was built in 1878-9. *Right:* Auction details for the Lodge, 1996. It has since been modernised.

A slight diversion from the Lodge gates brings us to Penley Banks, a medieval sunken hollow-way on the road to Ellesmere.

Left: Penley Bank Cottage, 1883, home to the Fowles family since before 1837. Thatched roof in evidence. L to r: Benjamin Fowles (46), Mary (13), Mary (59, sister), Louisa (6), Eliza (44, wife), John (3), Henry (9).

Right: The elaborate funeral card of Benjamin Fowles, who died 21 January 1893.
Below: Penley Bank Cottage, 1986, when Vincent Straczinski, Polish exile and part-time pig-farmer, was selling up. It has since been demolished and a new house built in its place.

LLANNERCH PANNA
and PENLEY HOUSE

With the eclipse of the Penley Hall dynasty, a new star was in the social ascendant, the Hon. George T. Kenyon, who in 1878-9 commissioned John Douglas, the Chester architect to design the Victorian 'Tudor' mansion house which he called Llannerch Panna (the Welsh name for Penley). It was situated alongside Penley House, where he had lived for several years before letting it as a 'hunting box'.

Above: Architect's front elevation of Llannerch Panna, February 1879. The service wing (with butler's pantry and servants' hall) and walled yard did not materialise. Instead a long corridor gave access to Penley House.
Below: The gardens and rear elevation of Llannerch Panna, 1879. The Hon. George married Florence Anne Leche of Carden Park, Cheshire and the design of Llannerch Panna is allegedly based on her Elizabethan half-timbered ancestral home, unfortunately largely destroyed by fire in 1912.

Left: The Hon. G.T. Kenyon and wife on the rear lawn of Llannerch Panna, 1890. The Hon. George was elected Conservative MP for the Denbigh Boroughs in 1885, 1886 and 1892 but lost his seat in the 1906 election. He was Chairman of the Wrexham & Ellesmere Railway and Junior Deputy-Chancellor of the University of Wales. He died at Llannerch Panna on 26 January 1908 following a road traffic accident.

Right: Mrs George Kenyon (1854-1929) feeding her pony at Llannerch Panna. She continued to farm the estate for some 20 years after her husband's death.
Below: Subscription List to the celebrations upon the safe return of the Hon. George and Mrs Kenyon from a round the world honeymoon in 1876.

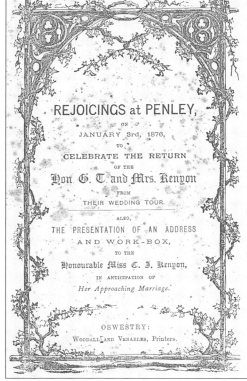

REJOICINGS at PENLEY,

ON

JANUARY 3rd, 1876,

TO

CELEBRATE THE RETURN

OF THE

Hon G. T. and Mrs. Kenyon

FROM

THEIR WEDDING TOUR.

ALSO,

THE PRESENTATION OF AN ADDRESS
AND WORK-BOX,

TO THE

Honourable Miss C. J. Kenyon,

IN ANTICIPATION OF

Her Approaching Marriage.

OSWESTRY:
WOODALL AND VENABLES, Printers.

List of Subscribers.

	£	s.	d.		£	s.	d
Earl Brownlow ...	5	0	0	Mr. J. Williams	0	10	0
Mrs. Dymock ...	5	0	0	,, T. N. Williams	0	10	0
Ormsby Gore, Esq., M.P.	3	0	0	,, W. Ashley	0	5	0
S. K. Mainwaring, Esq.	3	0	0	,, W. Bennett	0	5	0
Hon. R. W. S. Cotton	2	0	0	,, E. K. Bickley	0	5	0
Major Cust, M.P.	2	0	0	,, J. Carr	0	5	0
R. M. Dymock, Esq.	2	2	0	,, C. Cooke	0	5	0
J. Jones, Esq.	2	0	0	,, R. Copnall	0	5	0
Mr. T. Griffiths,	2	0	0	,, B. Egerton	0	5	0
R. G. Jebb, Esq.	1	0	0	,, W. Highway	0	5	0
T. J. Provis, Esq.	1	0	0	,, J. Hotchkins	0	5	0
Major Playne Smith	1	0	0	,, W. Hughes	0	5	0
Mr. T. Williams	1	1	0	,, J. Humphreys	0	5	0
,, E. Alderman	1	0	0	,, F. Jones	0	5	0
,, J. Ashley	1	0	0	,, Jones	0	5	0
Mrs. Capper	1	0	0	,, J. Kendall	0	5	0
Rev. R. W. Foulger	1	0	0	,, R. Matthews	0	5	0
Mr J. Hayward ...	1	0	0	,, Morgan	0	5	0
,, A. Key	1	0	0	,, J. Norton	0	5	0
,, W. Lee	1	0	0	,, J. Pay	0	5	0
,, Wycherley	1	0	0	,, J. Pemberton	0	5	0
,, W. Woodall	1	0	0	,, J. Phillips	0	5	0
,, J. Ashley	0	10	6	,, T. Reeves	0	5	0
,, E. Hayward	0	10	6	,, C. Roberts	0	5	0
,, W. Mair	0	10	0	Mrs. Roberts	0	5	0
,, J. Allinson	0	10	0	Mr. J. Rodenhurst	0	5	0
,, J. Broomhall	0	10	0	,, C. Sparrow	0	5	0
,, A. Chidlow	0	10	0	,, L. Thomas	0	5	0
,, W. Clay	0	10	0	,, R. Tomson	0	5	0
,, J. Davies	0	10	0	Mrs. Townsend	0	5	0
Messrs. Dawson & Owen	0	10	0	,, Vaughan	0	5	0
Mr. G. George	0	10	0	Mr. A. Williams	0	5	0
,, G. Griffiths	0	10	0	,, G. Williams	0	5	0
,, W. Griffiths	0	10	0	,, J. Williams	0	5	0
,, J. Hayward, jun.	0	10	0	,, W. Wilson	0	5	0
,, S. Hopley	0	10	0	Mrs. Woolrich	0	5	0
,, R. Hughes	0	10	0	Mr. Cooke	0	2	6
,, T. Hughes	0	10	0	Mrs. Davies	0	2	6
,, J. Jones	0	10	0	Mr. G. Davies	0	2	6
,, J. Jones	0	10	0	,, W. Griffiths	0	2	6
,, J. Kelsall	0	10	0	,, E. Jones	0	2	6
,, F. Lee	0	10	0	,, S. Martin	0	2	6
,, T. Lunt	0	10	0	,, C. Williams	0	2	6
,, S. Maddocks	0	10	0	,, W. Wilson	0	2	6
Dr. Moorhouse	0	10	0	,, J. Chesters	0	2	0
Mr. J. Nunnerley	0	10	0	,, J. Leadson	0	2	0
Dr. Roe	0	10	0	,, J. Hughes	0	1	0
Mr. G. Rodenhurst	0	10	0	,, J. Kelly	0	1	0
,, J. Steele	0	10	0	,, W. Simons	0	1	0
				,, J. Wynne	0	1	0

It should here be stated that our Churchwarden, Mr. R. Allen, had subscribed to the Hanmer branch of the rejoicings before he was aware of any steps being taken at Penley to celebrate the event. Hence his name does not appear in this list.

Above: Llannerch Panna, 1929, as seen in the auction catalogue of 17 September, when the estate was put up for sale following the death of Mrs. Kenyon. As built, the house varies in detail from the architect's original plan. At this time 59 acres remained attached to the house but it was withdrawn at £4,400, but was eventually bought by Miss Gwendoline Leche of Carden Hall, Mrs. Kenyon's half-sister.
Right: Detail of Lot 1 (Llannerch Panna) from the auction catalogue, 1929.

LOT 1.

LLANERCH PANNA.

A Charming Country Residence,

designed upon a 16th Century Model and standing in a position of great sylvan beauty in the fertile " Hundred of Maelor," 3 miles from Ellesmere and about midway between Wrexham and Whitchurch.

EARLY POSSESSION.

This distinctive Residence is approached by a fine avenued Drive from the Main Road, is fronted by a small cobbled Forecourt, and a rectangular Grass Plot mounted by an antique Sun Dial.

The Entrance is guarded by an Oak doored Entrance Hall, opening into a lofty and expansive Galleried Lounge Hall, Oak Panelled Dining Room (approx. 18ft. by 21ft), Drawing Room (approx. 24ft. by 18ft.), Small Study (Lavatory), Staircase Hall.

The Principal Bedrooms lead off the Gallery which is sufficiently spacious to allow for a cosy Fireplace and Two Alcoves. They comprise :—

Bedroom (approx. 21ft. by 18ft), Dressing Room (10ft. by 10ft), 3 Smaller Bedrooms.

Landing with Two Wardrobes.

Single Bedroom, Lavatory and W.C., Housemaid's Cupboard, Linen and China Cupboards.

On a lower floor are two Large Bedrooms, and two Smaller ones, and Boxroom approached by Secondary Staircase.

The Domestic Apartments are pleasantly arranged and include Housekeeper's Room, Servants' Hall, Kitchen, Larder and Scullery.

Wine Cellar.

LIVERPOOL CORPORATION'S WATER SUPPLY is laid on.

THE GROUNDS are delightfully placed and are studded by a variety of Ornamental Trees which have a very beautiful effect. The Terraced Lawns and the natural fall of the Grounds lend themselves to artistic treatment and although at present they do not show themselves to advantage, their suitability for development at little cost, is apparent. The Sylvan Slope in the West leads down to a levelled space which is delightfully placed and has often been the scene of Dancing Parties.

THE WALLED GARDEN
(with Potting Shed)

has a convenient position and **THE ORCHARD** has a Sunny aspect.

Above: Miss Leche made several alterations to the house, notable separating the old 'Penley House' from the building and adding a new domestic wing, seen here on the left in 1953, when Llannerch Panna was once more put up for sale.

Right: Herbert Williams and John Thomas Lunt, gardeners at Llannerch Panna, 1950.

Before Llannerch Panna there was 'Penley House', a substantial freehold residence and farm (100 acres), built c.1842 on the site of the even older 'Fields House'. This was sold to the Hon. George Kenyon in 1874, a year or so before his marriage. He would eventually use Penley House as the servants wing to Llannerch Panna and it remained as such until 1930, when it was once more made a separate building, albeit reduced somewhat in size.

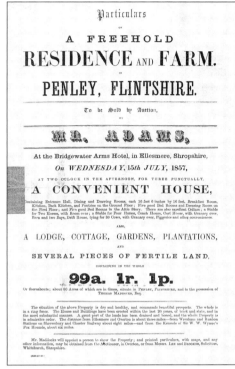

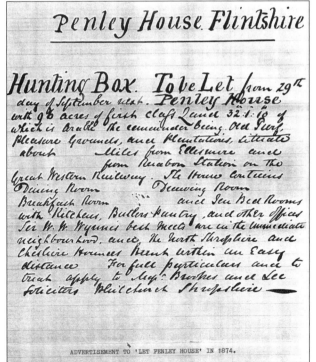

Top left: Llannerch Panna Cottage, aka Penley House in 1970. Even as a 'cottage' it is not difficult to picture this house as a former 10-bedroom mansion.

Top right: Details of Penley House auction, 1857. Bought as an investment by John Vernon, Tushingham, Malpas.

Left: Until he had built Llannerch Panna, the Hon. George Kenyon was content to let Penley House as a 'hunting box'. This draft advertisement of 1874 extols the sporting advantages of the house.

Left: Llannerch Panna Cottage, 1953, winner of the 'Best Dressed House in Penley' Competition in Coronation year, for Harry and Florence Dutton.

Left: Llannerch Panna Cottage taken from the drive, March 1977, before the large tree was felled.

Bottom left: Llannerch Panna Cottage, 1985. Much reduced from when it was built as Penley House in 1842, it is still an impressive pile.

Bottom right: Penley House was last sold in 2000. Even now it boasts six bedrooms, two stable blocks and 2 acres of paddocks and gardens. Some cottage!

In the latter part of 1942, as part of Operation Bolero, code name for the building up of an American military presence in this country, a cluster of five US Army hospitals sprouted on green sites straddling the Flintshire Maelor-north Shropshire border. The camps built at Oteley Hall, Ellesmere and Halston Hall, Whittington, near Oswestry were dual purpose 'conversion' units which could, and did become hospitals. The largest hospital (1500 beds) was built in the grounds of Iscoyd Park, near Whitchurch. Penley's two 'great houses' were also requisitioned. No.83 Station Hospital with 800 beds was built in the grounds of Llannerch Panna This also staffed outlying aid-stations around Wrexham, e.g. the US Army camp at Plas Power. No.129 General Hospital (1000 beds) took up its three year residency at Penley Hall and would handle over 10,000 battle casualties before disbanding in July 1945 after laying up its colours in Wrexham parish church.

Both Penley hospitals were built by Sir Robert McAlpine & Sons, Ltd and each cost near enough the same - £25,000. The three Maelor hospitals formed a 'hospital centre', between them catering for every type of war casualty. They were the northernmost units served by hospital trains from the Channel ports, or immediately after D-day, by Casevac Dakotas flying into conveniently placed RAF aerodromes at Rednal, Sleap and Whitchurch. Almost overnight the population of Penley trebled, its inhabitants subject to a sustained cultural battering as they tried to adjust to the weird and wonderful life style and seeming extravagances of their uninvited guests. Impact on the farming landscape was total as a rash of wards and barracks spread either side of Big Green and lanes and tracks were upgraded (at no expenses to the ratepayers of Overton RDC) to handle the hospital generated traffic. Public utilities such as electricity and sewerage were experienced for the first time.

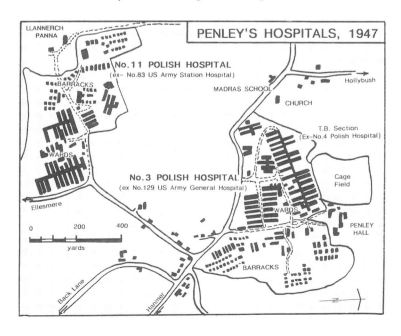

Map showing locations of the two American military hospitals in Penley. It is clear that they swamped the Big Green area of the tiny 'native' village.

The parkland of Penley Hall (right centre), between Church Green and Big Green, was requisitioned for No.129 US Army General Hospital. There was no attempt at camouflage, air raids on Merseyside having petered out by August 1942. The impact on a virtually medieval rural landscape is immediately evident. (Copyright, CPAT 1984)

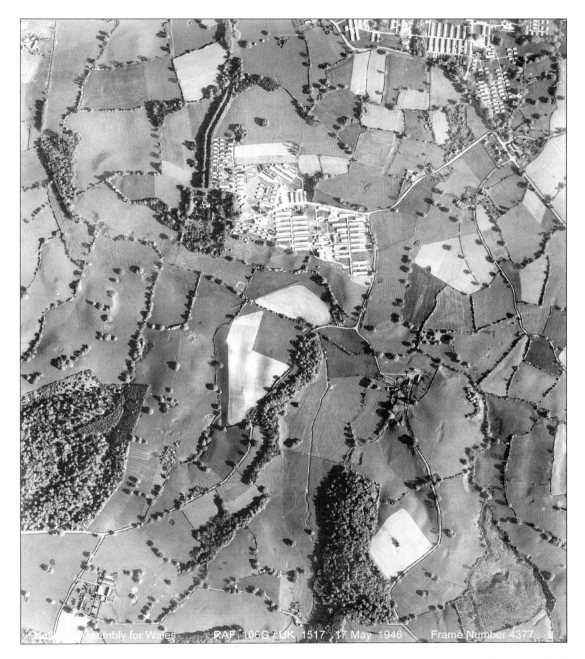

Barely 100 yards from the Shropshire border No.83 Station Hospital was planted in the grounds of Llannerch Panna (visible in the block of trees). (Crown Copyright, National Assembly for Wales)

Being a US Army installation, not many wartime images of the Penley hospitals survive in local archives. This rare picture, dating from 1944/5 shows No.83 Station Hospital, Llannerch Panna, taken from the top of the water tower. Long buildings are the wards. The smaller huts to the rear are nurses' and doctors' quarters. Enlisted men (support personnel) are quartered out in front of the poplar trees which line the front drive to Llannerch Panna.

The third US Army hospital built in Maelor was located at Iscoyd Park on the England/Wales border, three miles west of Whitchurch, Shropshire, staging post for both hospital trains and Casevac Dakota aircraft. With the two Penley hospitals it formed a 'hospital centre', able to treat every possible combination of battlefield injury. (Crown Copyright, National Assembly for Wales)

Above: Volleyball match between Nos. 3 and 4 Polish Hospitals, 1950. Played at Iscoyd Park.

Below: Polish soccer team, Iscoyd Park, 1954-5. Made up of medical and ancillary staff. Back row, l-r: 1. Derek Bell, 6. Jan Zamojski, 7 Berwyn Morris. Front row, l-r: J. Kielbinski, Mr. Wajda, Dr.Rogalski, Z. Zamojski, Mr. Hollweger.

Above: Polish dancing group at Iscoyd Park, 1954. The last hospital fete before closure.

Below: Another season's soccer team, Iscoyd Park, 1952-3. Back row, l-r: 1. August ('Johnny) Bera, 2. Jan Zamojski, 5. Derek Bell, 6. Berwyn Morris. Front row, l-r: 3. Z. Zamojski.

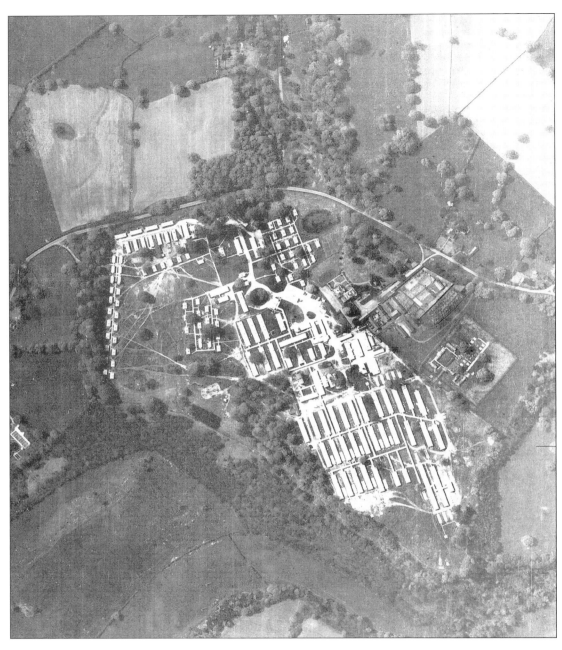

An enlargement of the US Army Hospital at Iscoyd Park, fronting the hall and home farm. Seen here on 2 May 1946, on care and maintenance, just before the arrival of the Polish Resettlement Corps. (Crown Copyright, National Assembly for Wales)

(163) Unlike the two Penley hospitals which lingered on to the present time, as soon as No.4 Polish Hospital, Iscoyd Hall, was declared redundant and all TB patients moved to Penley in 1955, the wartime hospital was cleared, the site reverting to parkland and a cricket oval. This photo was taken on 22 March 1972, but 'crop marks' indicative of former hut foundations may be seen under, and to the NE of the cricket ground. (Crown Copyright, National Assembly for Wales)

Of the two Polish hospitals in Penley, No.11(bottom) was the smaller and would close first. In March 1954 proposals to convert it into an Open Prison were abandoned, as were subsequent plans by a private developer for storage units and/or a permanent caravan site. (Crown Copyright, National Assembly for Wales)

Above: Poles did their best to make an old Army camp seem like home. Mr. Jan Zamojski in his rose garden on Llannerch Panna, 1949.

Left: But it was still run on semi-military lines. Mr. Jan Zamojski collects a mug of tea and plate of 'sausage and mash' from the canteen, 1948.

Even in war and as refugees the Poles were ever ready to make music. Resettlement Corps orchestra at a Llannerch Panna garden party, 1948.

Above: Somewhere in Scotland, 1945, after disembarkation from Italy. Polish Forces band, some of whom would find their way to Penley. 3rd row, 2nd left, Jan Zamojski.

Below: A slightly more informal band, Scotland 1945. They played at local dances.

Above: By 1952, troubles of war and resettlement behind them, there had emerged in Penley a 'hot' little sextet, Polskie Echo. From l-r: Mr. Holweger, Walter Holweger, unknown, Mr. Theur, Stefan Jacelski, Jan Zamojski.

Below: The ability to play an instrument came in handy. Guard of honour at military funeral, Ellesmere Cemetery, June 1946.

Llannerch Panna Hospital site in 1964. Frustrated by the rejection of his plans the developer offered the site for piecemeal salvage and extraction of hard-core etc. For years the site took on a derelict air, a blot on the landscape, until taken over for housing in the 1980s. Here secondary self-seeding vegetation colonises what is left of some of the wards.

Forlorn relic of a ward, No.11 Polish Hospital, Llannerch Panna, 1965.

No.11 Polish Hospital, looking across the silent MT Square to the derelict wards.

EWS tank, Llannerch Panna, 1965, but disused since the American occupation of the camp.

1970 marked the redevelopment of the former No.11 Polish Hospital site on Llannerch Panna. The former ward area was the first to emerge as a modern housing estate, Hill Crest to the foreground, the E-W line of trees marking the course of the Vyrnwy-Liverpool aqueduct, Oak Drive beyond, with the Ellesmere Lane curving away, centre right.

Above: One of the last 'resident' line inspectors for NW Water holds a watching brief on Llannerch Panna as new estate drainage works is carried across the Liverpool aqueduct. Beyond the pile of rubble from demolished hospital water tower the skeletal frameworks of one of the old wards.

Left: Damage to new housing as a result of freak gales, October-November 1971. A 12ft section of wall crumpled when rammed by a flying garage roof. The alignment of Penley Brook can, under certain circumstances, make for strong anabatic air currents accompanied by considerable turbulence on top of the valley side.

The post-1945 history of Poland needs no repetition in a work of local history. Suffice it to say that at the end of the war there was no enforced repatriation of Poles. Of their own volition some 105,000 Poles returned to their native land, France accepted 7,000, while 14,000 emigrated to other countries, leaving some 150,000 Polish servicemen and women who preferred to remain in the UK. By the Resettlement Act of 1947, the Polish Armed Forces were disbanded to reform almost immediately into the Polish Resettlement Corps (PRC) which in turn would be disbanded in 1949, having achieved its principal objective of integrating Poles into British society. The problem was exacerbated by the thousands of Polish Displaced Persons, ex POWs, political prisoners, forced labour etc. from the refugee and concentration camps of Germany

The Polish eagle flew over No.3 Polish Hospital on Polish national days and the great religious festivals.

who were admitted into the UK as European Volunteer Workers. The huge numbers involved meant that the Poles in exile had to be accommodated in camps and hostels widely dispersed so as to minimise impact upon local communities, commencing with six camps housing 4,000 Poles in August 1947 but rising to 99 camps with 25,000 Poles in residence by October 1948. In NE Wales and border counties one can recall national assistance board camps at Wynnstay Park, Oulton Park, Perton, Rednal, Penrhos, Tilstock (Prees), The Hermitage (Wrexham), Hawarden, Doddington, Calveley, many of these ex-Army or RAF camps. The three former US Army hospitals in Maelor mustered some 2,000 beds for the treatment of an immigrant population that had suffered five years of harsh treatment and deprivations. Tuberculosis was a particular problem until the 1960s. No.3 Polish General Hospital had followed the Polish 2nd Corps throughout the North African and Italian campaigns of the British 8th Army, ending up in Palagiano before embarking from Senigalia for the UK. 31% of doctors and 24% of its nurses ended up at Penley as did, by coincidence?, No. 3 Polish Hospital.

The former No.129 US Army Hospital in the grounds of Penley Hall, May 1946, when under 'care and maintenance'. Within the year it would become No. 3 Polish Hospital. East (right) of the main drive are staff married quarters, kitchens and motor pool. The central block of wards are currently (May 2003) being replaced by a new hospital. The westernmost wards have been converted into Penley Industrial Estate. Note, north of the hospital and south of the sewage plant a small hutted compound in the Cage Field - a small German POW camp under American control.

Top left: 1942. Polish soldiers get fit and well on the shores of the Caspian Sea, Persia, after being released from Russian internment camps.

Top right: Left: a rather emaciated Piotr Sadowski in Persia, four weeks after his release from Russian captivity, 1942. Five years later Piotr ended up in Penley and married a local girl.

Below: Polish soldiers dug in at Tobruk, 1943.

Left: Piotr Sadowski left, now promoted sierzant, as a member of the Carpathian Brigade, Tobruk, 1943.

Below: The monastery at Monte Cassino, Italy, symbol of German resistance to the Allied advance up Italy. It finally fell to Polish forces on 18 May 1944, but not without heavy casualties.

Left: After the battle came the awards for bravery. Sierzant Piotr Sadowski, left, has been awarded
the Virtute Militari (the highest Polish award), the Cross of Valour and the Monti Cassino Medal.

Right: The Polish brigades had their own field hospitals in Italy. Surgeons at work during the battle for Monti Cassino, 1944.

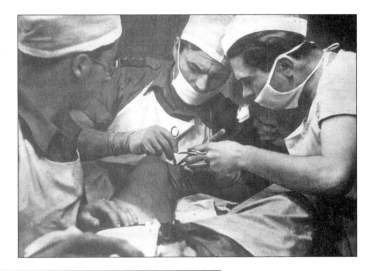

Left: A wounded soldier is stretchered away to a field hospital.

Right: Aftermath of the battle of the Metauro river, when Allies broke the Gothic Line, summer 1944. Surgeons battle to save a man's leg.

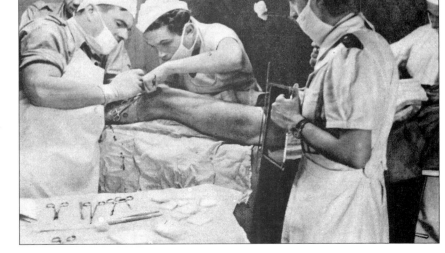

Doctors of the 3rd Polish General Hospital, Palagiano, Italy, 1945. Eleven of these pictured would later work at Penley.

Nursing staff, 3rd Polish General Hospital, Palagiano, Italy, 1945. Some sixteen of these later served at Penley.

Above: Doctors, surgeons and pharmacists, 3rd Polish General Hospital, Senigalia, Adriatic Coast, before embarking for the UK and Penley.
Below: A male ward, No.3 Polish Hospital, 1950. Doctors' rounds in progress. Still highly regimented with patients 'sitting by their beds'. The coke stove and polished bitumastic floors, which gave problems in warm weather, were inherited from the Americans.

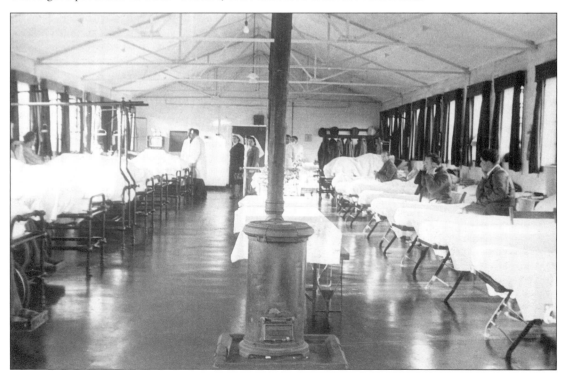

Above: No mistaking the hospital's military provenance. Stark hutted wards, No.3. Polish Hospital, Penley Hall, in 1950.

Below: Less like an Army camp. By 1965 harsh lines had been blurred by the laying out of ornamental grounds with shrubs and flower beds. View looking north from main gate, admin., records, single staff accommodation to left, motor pool, fire station and store to right.

Above: Looking south towards main gate, with Maelor School beyond, 1965. Admin. buildings on right, maintenance services (electrical, mechanical) on left.

Below: Immaculate grounds, 1965. The wards in the background were the last part of the hospital to function before closure in 2002.

One of a series of postcards of the Polish Hospital produced in 1958 by Mr. Wernik. In background, Staff Social Club with invalid car garages to left, hospital and RC chapel to right.

Above: The Polish RC chapel, 1950. Formerly the American garrison church. Altar and reredos were carved and painted by Polish craftsmen. Latterly the chapel was housed in a redundant ward in the main hospital complex. It has now closed and its furnishings have gone to Penrhos Polish village in the Lleyn Peninsula.

Left: Wherever located, prominent in the Polish chapel was this image of Our Lady of Ostrabrama, made by Polish soldiers from empty coffee tins in the Military Hospital at El Kantara in 1943.

Above: Feast of Corpus Christi, 12 June 1952. The religious procession has just left the chapel and is heading down the main drive of the hospital, possibly to tour the wards.

Right: Feast of Corpus Christi, 1952. The weather is fine and to allow patients in wheelchairs to attend the Mass an altar has been set up outside the chapel, beautifully decorated, with the image of Our Lady of Ostrabrama prominent.

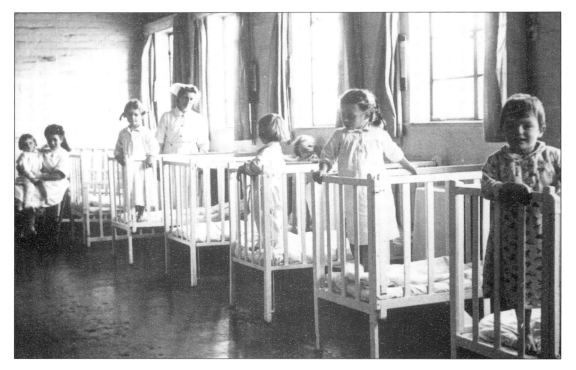

Above: The Children's Ward, No.3 Polish Hospital, Penley, 1949. Staff midwife Klepaka, standing; nursing auxiliary Walaszek, sitting. These children are fortunate. Penley churchyard contains the graves of some 62 'Polish babies', buried between November 1946 and 1954, aged anything from 8 hours to three days.
Below: The Nursery, 1955. Hospital staff could leave their children here whilst they were working. Staff midwife Klepacka in background.

Right: No.3 Polish Hospital was very well equipped, courtesy of the US Army. Serious cases were, of course, treated at the War Memorial Hospital, Wrexham. A corner of the operating theatre, 1950.

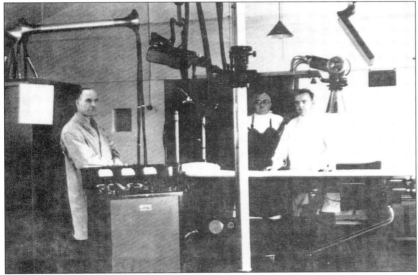

Left: The X-ray Department, 1950. Mr. Szamaza, radiographer, far right.

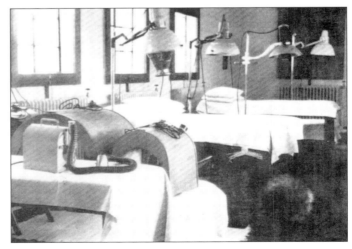

Right: The Physiotherapy Department, 1950.

Above: Carpentry Workshop, 1950; used for occupational therapy and for teaching of new skills that might prove useful in the general integration process. The Penley workshops were on a partial business footing. Patients, who had been experienced woodworkers in civilian life, were often commissioned to produce and repair items of furniture for local people.
Below: Cobblers' Workshop, 1950. Old skills revised, new skills learnt. Polish craftsmen kept the whole of Penley well shod!

Above: The hospital kitchens 1950, with food trolleys being recharged; demolished along with original staff dining rooms, as the hospital retrenched in the 1980s.

Below: How meals were taken to patients on the wards; Mr. Jan Zamojski, right, and another unidentified nursing auxiliary return food trolley to the kitchens, August 1951.

Above: The hospital cinema, complete with proper cinema seats, was inherited from the Americans, but in 1950 was run by the AKC. It could screen full-size 35mm films, while a portable 16mm projector and screen could take films around the wards.

Below: Patients' games room, 1950. The full-sized snooker table was inherited from the Americans, along with the heating stove! Staff had their own recreation room and table.

Above: No.3 Polish Hospital archery team returns with a trophy, 1950, won at the Stoke Mandeville International Games for the disabled.

Below: A Penley wheelchair javelin thrower warms up under the careful eye of Mr. Cyran, physiotherapist, left, and carer Jan Zamojski, at Stoke Mandeville Games, early 1950s.

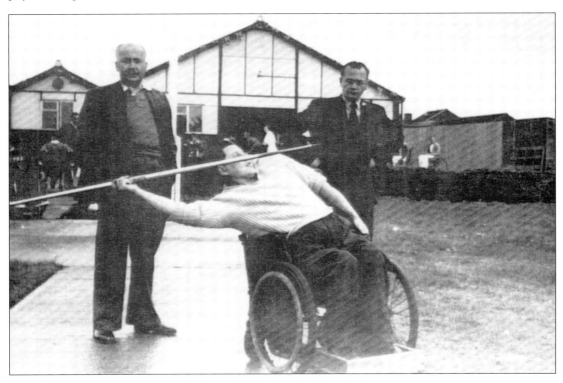

Above: Polish Amateur Dramatics, 1952. Teresa Mordok, second right.

Below: ADS Chorus, give a concert of Polish folk songs, 1953.

Amateur Dramatics, 1953. 3rd left: Gertruda Puszkiewicz; 2nd right: Kasza Kosjak; 3rd right: Mrs Chwalibog. The latter, who worked in the pathology department, ran the Polish 'Sunday School', teaching Polish language, culture and heritage.

Above: 1953 ADS production. Back row from left: 1. Antoni Grigierczyk; 3. Tadeusz Sosinski; 4. Eva Renka. Front row from left: Kasza Kosjak; Gertruda Puszkiewicz; Jan Zamojski.

Below: ADS photo-call 1953. The entire cast of A Krakow Wedding.

A rather boisterous wedding reception for Antoni and Janina Grygierczyk, bride just coming through the door; groom standing below the accordion player. Another booking for Polskie Echo.

Possibly out of nostalgia, hospital staff ran a Polish folk dancing troupe which gave displays locally and further afield at Llangollen and Blackpool. Conversely, dancing groups and choirs from Manchester, Bradford and other industrial towns where Poles had settled in numbers, would visit Penley to entertain the patients. Here the Penley Hospital troupe, with a 'Carpathian' backing group of two clarinets, violin, accordian and drums.

Above: Penley Polish Folk Dancing Group are seen leaving the competition field at the Llangollen International Eisteddfod, June 1954.

Below: Three Polish dancers at Penley, 1953; from the portrait in the background, obviously celebrating the Coronation of Queen Elizabeth II.

The Penley Polish dancing team that competed at Llangollen in 1954. Back row from left: 1. Mr. Czaglinski; 2. Mr. Pushalski; 3. Olgerd Kielbinski; 4. Dr. Rogalski; 5. Mr. Theur; 6. Jan Zamojski; 7. Mr. Zaniewski.

Penley Polish dancers give a display for the Polish community at Blackpool, 1954, which town had strong wartime links with the Polish Air Force in exile., hosting aircrew reception and trade training centres.

Left: The Staff Social Club was the venue for regular dances. Polish hospitality was noted far and wide. A happy group in the run up to Christmas, 1965. From left: Antoni Grygierzyk, Janina Grygierzyk, Tadeuz Sosinski, Gertruda Sosinska, Weronika Doryn, Adam Doryn.

Right: By this time Polskie Echo had given way to Dick Cross's Overton-based Savana Band with from left: Jan Zamojski (trumpet), Dick Cross (drums), Gordon Fowles (saxophone), Kathleen Hamlington (accordion) and Gwen Daulby (piano).

Below: The children have their own party, slightly more spartan!

Above: Second generation Polish teenagers, born and bred at the hospital, entertain the patients, Christmas 1965.

Below: Younger children give a Polish version of the Christmas story, complete with Polish carols, 1965. Almost hidden, far left, the shadowy figure of Mrs. Chwalibog, carrier of the flame for Polish language and traditions.

Above: Echoes of war some twenty years later. Old soldiers are visited by a retired Polish general. On such occasions wartime ranks were much in evidence. Left: (Colonel) Dr. Bereza, medical administrator; centre: (Col.) Soboniewski (general's aide); shaking hands with patient: General Rudnicki.

Below: More informal was the visit of the Mayor of Wrexham in 1966.

Inevitably, as Poles were assimilated into the community at large, the days of No.3 Polish Hospital were numbered. Retrenchment had begun in 1960 when part of the hospital site was sold for housing. This aerial view taken in 1993 shows the inroads made by Dymock Place and Penda's Park. Staff accommodation and former enlisted men's hutments have been cleared to footings and are reverting to scrubland.

Above: Penley Hospital from the NW, near enough intact in 1984. The western (right-hand) section is being taken over piecemeal by light industry, but is yet to become an 'industrial park'. (Copyright, CPAT 84-8-18)

Below: Close up of the camp in 1984. Top centre: Penley Hall and farm buildings await clearance (1990) in their turn. The small sewerage works were installed by the US Army in 1942, but now serve the whole of Penley and much beyond, and have underpinned the 1980s expansion of the village. (Copyright, CPAT 84-8-19)

What is left of No.3 Polish Hospital in 1996. MT square, stores and kitchens have disappeared under housing. Behind the screen of trees to the left of the main gate, a dozen or so wards (buildings 45-57) have disappeared, just footings left. The group of 12 buildings (centre top), house admin, three wards, chapel stores, boiler house, kitchen, staff dining room, and maintenance work shop and will form the core of the hospital until closure in 2002.

Left: First part of the hospital to become redundant were the married quarters' hutments, with military style ablutions and toilet blocks. Seen here, behind Mary Rodenhurst and her bicycle, in 1950, in almost 'pristine' condition.

Below: The houses in Dymock Place were completed in 1961, the small council estate taking up a block of hospital land occupied by workshops. The gardens of No.7 afford a view of near derelict married quarters, dominated by the great landmark water tower.

Right: 1993, an air of dereliction everywhere as the hospital retrenches. Derelict wards on left of main drive.

Middle: 1988, cows graze on former MT square, surrounded by former stores, garages, fire station, etc.

Bottom: Abandoned Staff Social Club building is symptomatic of the gradual run down.

Above: Land east (right) of the main drive was the first earmarked for re-development. The hospital chapel, in 1993 approached by overgrown path and neglected flower beds, is scheduled to be moved into the main hospital complex on the other side of the drive.

Below: In 1993 the new water tower and twin stacks of the makeshift boiler house mark the concentration of medical and support services west of the main drive.

Above: Buildings 4-16 only survive in 1993. Catering and laundry departments occupy building on right, the wards, set back, will gradually reduce to one at closure.
Below: The surviving wards in 1993 have had a much needed coat of paint, but even these are closing until only Ward 7 is left.

Above: Buildings 45-55 (odd numbers) lined up for the demolition man in 1993. From the large double doors let into the ends of some of them they have obviously been re-cycled as storage buildings.

Left: The same buildings viewed from the other side where some wards and living quarters have already disappeared. Water tower and stoke hole are on building No.55.

Below: The footings of building No.56.

Right: 1993. Looking west over the little brook that divided the hospital, at the former TB section, established with the closure and transfer to Penley of No.4 Polish Hospital, Iscoyd Park in 1955. The buildings here have survived to the present day, recycled as small business units on Penley's tiny 'Industrial Estate'.

Left: Buildings 36 and 37, once the cook-house for this part of the hospital.

Right: Buildings 39 and 40 (water tower) were the former boiler house which heated some 16 wards plus auxiliary storage and maintenance hutments.

Above: Building 29, former double ward block, now given over to several light industrial units, 1993.
Below: Buildings 32 (wards), 27 (heating plant), 29 and 28 (wards) viewed from the churchyard, 1993.

Above: The main road, Penley 1962. A huge gap in the tree line, right, where the main gate to the hospital crashed through the trees.
Below: In 1960-61, ten years before a preservation order was slapped on remaining parkland trees, Dymock Place was built, leaving but a single tree; a grass verge has replaced park pale and ditch.

SE corner of the hospital grounds in 1993. This was the first part to be hived off for new housing. Penda's Park (right [1970s]) and (left) Oakwood Park. Hospital gate has been moved (bottom centre).

Above: Some idea of parkland lost to posterity may be gained by this image of Penley Hall gates in 1905.

Below: A little corner of parkland survived untouched until Penley Post Office and filling station were built. Here young men of the village gathered every Sunday after lunch for serious talk and the odd game of 'pitch and toss'. Here, from left: Lloyd Butler, Doug Rolfe, Gwilym Morris, Arch Rodenhurst, Berwyn Morris, Ronald Biggs and Cyril Armstrong.

Adjacent the hospital sewerage works is a 'moated homestead' site, its ditch much silted but still filled with water. It is one of possibly two in the parish and over 20 in Maelor as a whole. At 44 yards square it is large enough to hold medieval hall, barns, gardens, etc. (see map opposite) and is surrounded by the remnant 'ridge and furrow' of medieval strip farming. In other words it was a farm with a protective moat, where a 13th century ancestor of the Dymock family attacked and colonised the waste lands of Penley, the last vestiges of which disappeared only with the Enclosure Act of 1796. This particular moated site was badly damaged in the Civil War and was abandoned c.1645 for a more palatial dwelling at, first, Penley Old Hall then Penley Hall. (Copyright, CPAT)

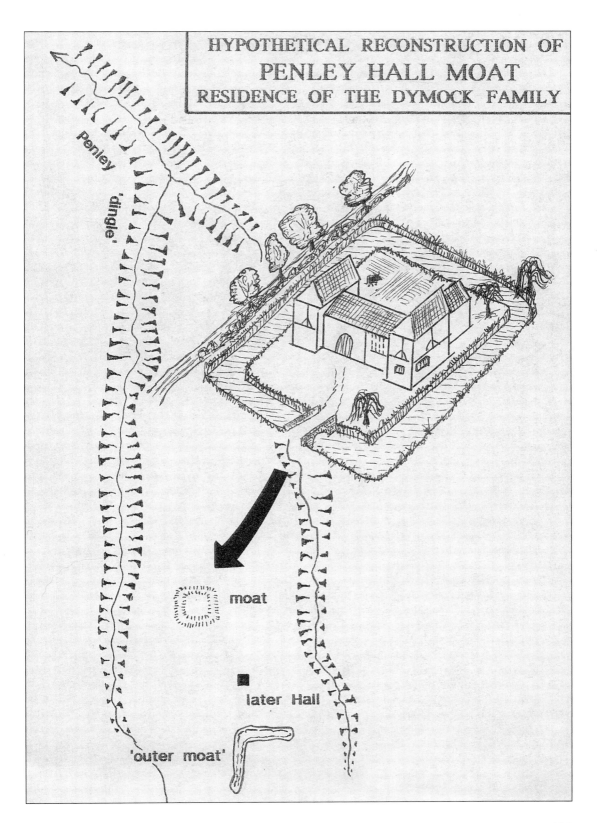

HYPOTHETICAL RECONSTRUCTION OF
PENLEY HALL MOAT
RESIDENCE OF THE DYMOCK FAMILY

Penley 'dingle'

moat

later Hall

'outer moat'

Penley Hall, 1905, a smallish Georgian mansion set in gardens and shrubberies with walled kitchen garden extending to 2.75 acres, along with a .337 acre pool. The hall itself contained: ground floor - large entrance hall with staircase, drawing room, dining room, staff room, kitchens, pantry and cellar; first floor - three bedrooms, dressing room, bathroom and a half landing to second floor - five further bedrooms, two boxrooms and a bathroom. There was a self-contained wing for staff quarters - living room, kitchen, three bedrooms and a bathroom. Outside there was a range of Georgian stables with two cottages, and even earlier half-timbered farm buildings, in addition to 95 acres of farmland, and 65 acres of woodland. Parkland extended to 39 acres, much as intake from Far Green or Big Green before the Enclosure Award of 1796.

Penley Hall c.1905; east elevation overlooking the gardens, dominated by a giant copper beech. When Robert Myddelton Dymock died in April 1899, aged 81 years, the Penley Hall estate passed to his nephew Theophilus Vaughton who adopted the surname Dymock, with the family hence known as 'Vaughton Dymock'. Theophilus immediately embarked upon the restoration of Penley Hall, which had been allowed to fall into disrepair. In 1900 three large bay windows were added, also a front porch which incorporated a frieze and drops of the stained-glass Dymock coats-of - arms from the 1784 parish church, demolished in 1899. Theophilus never lived in Penley, preferring Bath, where he died in 1905, aged 76 years. At this time Penley Hall was leased to Mr. and Mrs. Frank Cotton and family, who took up residence in May 1901. Miss V.E. Cotton surrendered the lease in March 1934.

Left: Few photographs seem to exist of the Dymocks of Penley Hall, but the family is recalled in memorials. The male line was snuffed out when Robert Townsend Dymock was killed in action on 17 October 1915. The west windows of Penley Parish Church, dedicated 16 March 1916, were erected to his memory.

Above: His eldest sister, Alice Louise Mary (1892-1984), ultimately (1949) inherited the Penley estates, which were gradually split up and sold. She is seen here in 1983 with four of her five children, three of whom have assumed the historic Dymock as a Christian name.

Right: The hatchment of Rev. Humphrey Dymock (1809-74), that hung in the 1784 church for some 25 years, still survives, having been returned to the family when that church was demolished.

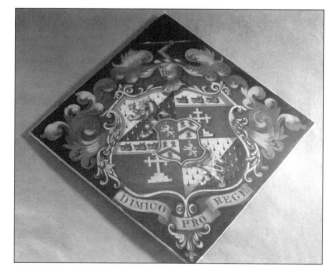

Left: The Dymock link with Penley is perpetuated by three vaults in the present churchyard. The second vault (1866-90) is in need of some careful conservation.

Below: The third vault (1874-91) is equally in need of attention. Its separate existence may hint at some ill-feeling between members of the family.

Below: The tombstones of Dafydd ap Madoc ap Ririd of Penley (top) and Gruffydd ab Iorwerth Foel of Halghton were found under the paved floor of Hanmer Church in 1857. Both were lost to posterity in the great fire of 1899. Dafydd ap Madoc (fl.mid-14th century) was the first to bear the anglicised name of 'Dymock'.

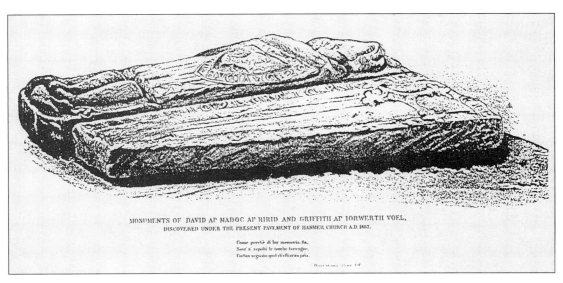

MONUMENTS OF DAVID AP MADOC AP RIRID AND GRIFFITH AP IORWERTH VOEL,
DISCOVERED UNDER THE PRESENT PAVEMENT OF HANMER CHURCH A.D. 1857.

Come perchè di lor memoria fia,
Sovr' a' sepolti le tombe terragne,
Portan segnato quel ch'elli eran pria.

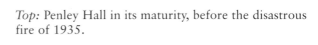

Top: Penley Hall in its maturity, before the disastrous fire of 1935.

Middle: Miss Violet Egerton Cotton, Penley Hall, at a Wynndstay Hunt meet at Iscoyd Park, 1922.

Bottom: Dr. John C. Clark, Cumbers Bank, 1910. From 1931 he and his wife lived at Penley Hall, companions to Miss Cotton.

Penley Hall was gutted by fire in the early hours of Tuesday, 26 February 1935. This photo shows the east elevation of the hall after the fire, with Bob Fletcher, groom, pointing to the window from which Miss Elizabeth Barnett, cook, was rescued by Reg Austin. Mrs. Constance Mostyn Owen, wife of Capt. Guy Mostyn Owen (current occupier of the hall), jumped from a 17ft window, suffering a severe shaking and bruised chin before raising the alarm and sprinting to the Post Office to summon the fire brigade....

(cont.).... Ellesmere and Whitchurch brigades attended. They could only contain the fire. Valuable oak panelling, much of it from the 1784 parish church, and a beautifully carved staircase of unknown provenance, were destroyed. Only the pieces of furniture that were dragged out by estate workers were saved. Total damage, covered by insurance, was estimated at some £4,500.

Left: Penley Hall, showing early signs of dilapidation in 1975. It had been occupied by hospital personnel since 1964.

Below: Even more dilapidated in 1986. The last occupant had been the Dowager Lady Kenyon. The Gredington Estate disposed of the hall to the Ministry of Works in 1964, who turned it into a dining room and kitchens for senior medical staff in the Polish Hospital. The hall had no place in the plans of the successor, Welsh Hospital Authority, and it was left to deteriorate further, before being sold to a private developer in 1986 and demolished the following year.

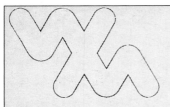

Wright-Manley

Surveyors. Land & Estate Agents. Auctioneers & Valuers

63 High Street
TARPORLEY
Cheshire CW6 0DR
Tel: (08293) 2151

6/8 Watergate Street
CHESTER
Cheshire CH1 2LA
Tel: (0244) 317833

128 Nantwich Road
CREWE
Cheshire CW2 6AU
Tel: (0270) 255396

Barker Street
CREWE
Cheshire CW2 6EG
Tel: (0270) 214301

55 High Street
NANTWICH
Cheshire CW5 5RP
Tel: (0270) 625410
& 625119

16 Watergate
WHITCHURCH
Shropshire SY13 1DX
Tel: (0948) 2281

40 Aston Street
WEM
Shropshire SY4 5AU
Tel: (0939) 32471

06G5316
06G5317

FOR SALE BY PRIVATE TREATY

Set in fine rural surroundings with open views, on the confines of the village of Penley, convenient for Wrexham 9 miles and Whitchurch about 8 miles.

An imposing Freehold Early Victorian Residence together with various other buildings, all with great potential for improvement or conversion having extensive grounds and extra land if required.

To be offered for Sale
in Two or more Lots, as required
known as

PENLEY HALL,
PENLEY, NEAR WREXHAM.

The availability of Penley Hall and associated buildings and land, on the open market, provides an exceptional opportunity for prospective purchasers to acquire property with considerable potential, either for conversion (subject to planning permission) or complete renovation. The property is approached from Whitchurch by turning right off the A539 into the Polish Hospital area (vehicular right-of-way) and then over the driveway through the grounds of the house.

Sale details for Penley Hall, 1986.

148

Top: Penley Hall was demolished in 1987. All that is left in 1993 are the former housekeeper's cottage, left, and the hall's back wall beyond. The grooms' 'Club Room' or bothy ('bothie'), has also gone, but the great bell that called generations of estate workers to and from their 12-hour work day fortunately survives in private hands.

Middle: The former housekeeper's cottage, seen here in 1993, has obviously been greatly modified.

Right: James and Kezia Davies, 1900. They lived at Penley Hall Cottage. Kezia was housekeeper to Mrs. Mary Vaughan Dymock, while James worked on Penley Hall Farm.

Above left: Adjacent to the mansion was Penley Hall Farm., home to the noted 'Penley Herd' of British Friesians, seen here in 1962.
Above right: The 'Penley Herd' in 1958, with farmer George Evans by his Land Rover. Tragically the entire herd would be wiped out in the 1967 outbreak of Foot and Mouth.

Right: But, although dilapidated, these farm buildings were timber-framed and therefore of some use to architectural restorers etc. The Penley Hall barn in 1988.

Left: The range of farm buildings in 1988, obsolete by current standards. Beyond stretch Penley Hall stables and dovecote, the latter ultimately salvaged and re-erected elsewhere in the former hall grounds.

Left: In 1990, after a winter of hurricane-force winds and a severe earth tremor in the April, demolition of the ancient farm buildings proceeded apace on public safety grounds. However, complete timber walls were salvaged and carefully dismantled by experts from Tarporley, Cheshire, for use elsewhere. The back wall of the barn, with timbers and joints marked for easier re-assembly.

Right: Likewise the gable end of the former shippons has been tagged ready for dismantling.

Left: The dismantling of the shippon back wall has started.

Above: Penley has its fair share of Elizabethan farm buildings, but appearance can be deceptive. In 1980, fronting a cobble yard (cobbles later salvaged) one sees only a range of shippons scarred by winter gales and no longer used for milking.

Right: To the rear and in the gable ends, timbers suggest an earlier function as a box-frame barn, 16.7 metres long, for the storage of grain, in two sections, separated by a drift house or cartway.

Left: The back wall of the shippon reveals a box frame 22.3 metres in length, but at one time longer, having lost 9.1 metres to a newer brick wall.

RANGLE TOWN

By 1796 Penley Hall parkland had been enlarged by adding a big chunk - intake - of the former Big or Far Green, but along the southern edge of this piece of common land squatters had also been nibbling away at the Green for almost two centuries, starting with Fields House or Big Green Farm, a 9-acre, later 29-acre holding, the latter name transferring in 1936 to the more modern farmhouse and outbuildings down Ellesmere Lane, leaving a timber framed and clad barn/shippon to stand alone amidst small pieces of ridge and furrow. Fronting Fields House was a track which gave access to seven of the poorest cottages in Penley - the 'ancient enclosures' - pre-dating the 1796 Enclosure Award, and, until 1929, tied cottages to the Llannerch Panna estate. Three of these had disappeared by 1871. Four were left by 1907, leaving an attenuated 'squatters' row' to survive in various states of disrepair until the 1990s. Today known tactfully to the Post Office as 'Lane End', this lane is still referred to by older inhabitants of Penley as Rangle Town, derived from the OE wrang = 'crooked, twisted in shape' or OE wrangel, wrengel = 'a crooked, twisted place'. In the 1881 Census it had gone slightly up-market with a short-lived attempt to change its name to Whitechapel Row, almost as if the Chapel at No.1 had been given a coat of limewash. It was back to Rangle Town in 1891. Electoral Rolls refer to Big Green, 1918-1939. Lane End enters the rate books in 1936 and would seem to be a happy compromise.

Rangle Town in 1972. No.1 is a former chapel (note stone in gable end). Behind, an ex-Army hut provides 'superior' accommodation in the garden of No.2; further on the silhouette of No.2 itself.

Above: No.1 Lane End, 1988. Until 1901 a Primitive Methodist Chapel, the Penley 'preaching house' of 1851, when it could sit 30, with 10 standing, and an average evening congregation of 28. Originally the cottage was not used exclusively for worship. In 1851 Edward Williams, deacon, notes 'a family reside in it'. The bedroom floor bisected the pointed chapel window, the outline of which is differentiated in the rendering of the gable wall, below the rounded dedication stone inscribed 'Jehovah Jireh 1819'.

Left: All that remains of the old chapel after demolition in 1994. It had been empty and much vandalised since 1979. Three new houses now occupy the site.

Above: No.2. Rangle Town (Lane End),
1902. Rose Evans and her mother, Emma,
standing in the doorway. The cottage
comprised kitchen, back kitchen, pantry,
larder and two bedrooms. There was a very
large garden.

Right: In the 1920s the Evans family moved
to No.1 Rangle Town. Seen here in 1931,
outside No.1, are Emma Evans (77) and
husband Charles Evans (79).

At the door of No.2 Rangle Town, 1920; Maria Cheresia, wife of Franciscus Gwellelmus Doex with children Karel and Evelyn. Front: Madeleine, Mary and Julie. The family were Belgian refugees, brought from London to Penley by the Hon. Mrs. Kenyon, Llannerch Panna in 1914.

Above: Nos.3 and 4 Rangle Town, 1993, after a bungled attempt at DIY site clearance.

Right: Mrs. Kate Edge outside No. 3 Rangle Town, 1948.

Above: Behind Rangle Town was Fields House, originally a 9-acre holding, seen here in 1943.

Right: In 1970 the old barn/ shippon was all that was left of Fields House.

Above: Nellie, John and Ethel Metcalfe, children of
William and Mary Metcalfe, outside Fields House, 1910.

Two other Metcalfe children, 1910.
Above: Hannah Metcalfe; *right:* William Metcalfe.

Top left: In 1929 Fields House passed into the hands of the Evison family. Here Tom Evison junior, with sheepdog 'Nell' in 1931.
Top right: 1930. Stan Evison stands amongst the chickens at Fields House.

Right: 1932. Mrs. Sophia Evison, Fields House, with Kathleen Evison (niece) and sons Tom and Stan.